A–Z guide to money

William Kay

A–Z guide to money

Constable London

First published in Great Britain 1983
by Constable and Company Limited
10 Orange Street London WC2H 7EG
Revised edition published 1986
Copyright © 1983 by William Kay
ISBN 0 09 467160 5
Set in Linotron Plantin 11pt
by Rowland Phototypesetting Limited
Bury St Edmunds, Suffolk
Printed in Great Britain
by St Edmundsbury Press Limited
Bury St Edmunds, Suffolk

British Library CIP data
Kay, William
A–Z guide to money – Rev ed.
1. Finance – Dictionaries
I. Title
332'.03'21   HG151

ISBN 0 09 467160 5

Acknowledgements

When I started compiling this book, I little realised how many sources I would need to turn to for help, guidance, encouragement and raw data.

I list on p. 281 the most useful books which I either drew on, or which best flesh out the entries in this volume. I am deeply grateful to Elfreda Powell of Constable for guiding me down the path, and for my literary agent John Pawsey for making sure I did not dawdle on the way!

I am indebted to Pamela Allen and Sue Thomas for giving me some invaluable source material, to Rosemary Clements for taking the trouble to read and comment on the manuscript, and to my former wife Deb for sharing the typing and the work of pasting almost 1,400 entries into alphabetical order. All the mistakes are, of course, my own, and I would be glad to hear from any reader who spots an error, or who feels that an item has been wrongly left out.

W.K.
1986

NB. *Cross-references are in italic*

ACAS See *Advisory, Conciliation and Arbitration Service*

Accelerator
A concept which Lord Keynes latched on to, to explain how higher consumption can lead to higher investment. If the factories cannot keep pace with demand, their owners will invest in extra factory space and new machines. That will put spending power in the hands of suppliers of factories and machines, so that they will be able to expand too. All this will draw in more workers, who will in turn have more money in their pockets. The process can, of course, work in reverse.

Accepting house
An accepting house is one of the top *Merchant banks* in the City. What it accepts are *Bills of exchange*. Once they have had this endorsement the bills are more readily traded round the City's *Discount market*, and they do not suffer such a big discount. The *Accepting Houses*, which have to be British-controlled, belong to the *Accepting Houses Committee*. This acts as a lobby for the merchant banks in putting their views to the Bank of England, the Treasury or the periodic Royal Commissions on the City.

Account
In *Bookkeeping*, an account is the record of *Transactions* of a particular type or relating to a particular person. They may be *Personal accounts*, *Real accounts* or *Nominal accounts*. In banking one customer may have a *Current account*, a *Deposit account* and a *Budget account*.

Accounting reference date
Under the 1976 Companies Act, all companies must tell the Registrar of Companies when its accounting reference date is. This is the date when the *Balance sheet* will be struck, for the accounting reference period which has ended then. The accounts must be submitted to the registrar as well as the shareholders.

Accumulated fund
This is the phrase used to describe the past profits amassed
by a *Non-profit-making organisation*. As it has payments and
receipts, like any business, inevitably there is a profit or a
loss after a period. The difference is that the accumulated
fund is really a by-product of such bodies, and it will be up
to the members to decide how to spend it.

Accumulation
A word used by followers of share *charts* to say that someone
has been buying.

Acid test
This is one of the ways of assessing a company's ability to
pay its debts. Its cash and near-cash, such as bank balances
and any holdings of *Gilts*, are added together and divided
by current liabilities. If the two are equal, the company is very
strong, but an answer of 0.5 would be reasonable. See also
Current ratio, *working capital ratio*.

Action for the Victims of Medical Accidents
An organisation offering help and information to people who
feel they have had a raw deal from the surgeon's knife (or
the chemist's pills, for that matter). AVMA will put you in
touch with doctors and lawyers who can give an opinion
on your case. The address is 135 Stockwell Road, London
SW9 9TN.

Activity index
It is one thing to notice that a share (or a whole stock market)
is on the rise. It is another matter if that rise has been caused
by a large or small volume of trading. In New York, Tokyo
and other stock markets the volume figures are shown each
day for each stock or share. In London a figure is given only
for the overall market volume, but it can still act as a guide
to how firm a trend is likely to be. These volume figures
are converted into activity indices to give a point of
comparison.

Actual
A term used in *Futures* markets. It refers to the actual
security, currency or deposit, as opposed to the *Futures
contract* relating to it. It is officially called a *Financial
instrument*.

Additional component
Part of the *State Pension* Scheme. Every pensioner collects
the Basic Component, but those who earned more than a
certain amount when they worked are given the additional
component, to cushion the fall in their incomes. As usual
with pension matters, the sums are hard. You take your best
20 years' annual pay, and divide each one by 52 to get a
weekly figure. Then subtract the current basic State pension
from each weekly figure. Add together the figures you are
left with, and divide the result by 20 to get an average.
Divide that average by four – and you have your additional
component. However, it does not take full effect until 1998.
Until then, instead of a *quarter* of average weekly pay, the
proportion is diluted. You take the number of years between
1978 and your date of retirement and multiply by 1¼. In
1988, for example, that will be $10 \times 1\frac{1}{4} = 12\frac{1}{2}$. So pensioners
retiring that year will get an additional component of 12½%
of the average pay figure. And you get credits from
contributions to previous State pension schemes. See
Pension.

Additional personal allowance for children
This is for single parents or guardians, or men whose wives
are totally handicapped. It is allowed in addition to the
normal *Personal allowance*, but it cannot be claimed at the
same time as the married man's personal allowance. The
children in question must be under 18 and dependent on
whoever is claiming the allowance.

Additional voluntary contribution
A way of topping up your *Occupational pension*, and one
which your employer may not offer. If he does, and you have

the cash to spare, it is a good way of saving because of the tax relief you get. But it is hedged by strict *Inland Revenue* rules which you should study closely before taking the plunge. See *Salary sacrifice*.

ADR See *American Depository Receipt*.

Advance
A banker's polite word for a *Loan*, whereby he advances you money.

Advance Corporation Tax See *Imputation tax*.

Advance/Decline line
This is a tool of Chartist analysis of stock markets. The line traces the tug-o'-war between rising and falling share prices. The number of shares which rise each day is logged, and from this is subtracted the number of falls. It can be a useful measure of what is happening across the market, as opposed to the share indices which concentrate on a minority. See *Charts, High/low indicator*.

Advisory, Conciliation and Arbitration Service
This body was set up by the government to help prevent industrial disputes. It has a statutory duty to look at every case which comes before an *Industrial tribunal*, and is also available to help prevent or settle strikes and other disputes at work. ACAS has offices throughout the country, but the head office is at Cleland House, Page Street, London SW1.

Afghani
The national currency of Afghanistan. Worth about 1p.

After-hours dealing
The *Stock Exchange* trades officially between 9 a.m. and 3.30 p.m., when the trading floor closes. That is the moment when closing prices are recorded. But stockbrokers often carry on dealing with one another by telephone after

they return to their offices, usually until about 5 p.m. This is called after-hours dealing, and can produce share prices radically different from the official close.

Age allowance
Anyone over 64 at the start of the *Tax year* in April is entitled to have his or her *Personal allowance* upgraded to the age allowance, which is about a third bigger. But there is an earnings trap. If your total taxable income is over a certain amount, the age allowance is reduced by two-thirds of the difference, until it comes back down to the rate of the appropriate *Married* or *Single person's allowance*.

Age Concern
This is one of several organisations offering help and information on financial matters for the over-60s. The head office is at Bernard Sunley House, 60 Pitcairn Road, Mitcham, Surrey. There are also offices in Northern Ireland, Scotland and Wales. See also *Employment Fellowship*, *Help the Aged* and the *Pre-Retirement Association of Great Britain and Northern Ireland*.

Agent
An agent is someone who acts on behalf of his or her client, and the agent's first duty is to that client by obtaining the best prices and protecting the client's assets.

AGM See *Annual General Meeting*.

Allotment letter
This is a letter from a company to tell you that you have been allotted a number of shares in that company. Hang on to it: until the *Share certificate* arrives, the allotment letter is your proof of ownership. See *Letter of indemnity*, *Renunciation*.

Allowance
Anything you are allowed is an allowance. Some parents call

their children's pocket money an allowance. More
importantly, there is a series of *Tax* allowances which can
be offset against income or profits. In that sense, an
allowance is very similar to a *Tax relief*.

All-risks insurance
This is an extra cover for your valuables, insuring them
against loss or theft wherever in the world you take them –
not just around the house. It is usually a supplement to
Household insurance.

Alternate demand
Demand for goods which meet similar needs. The demand
alternates according to shifts in quality and price because
the goods can be easily substituted for one another. Different
types of meats are an example, as are competing brands
of soap powder or ice lollies.

Alternative investment
Alternative, that is, to conventional types of investment.
The alternatives are generally objects which go up and down
in value – antiques, diamonds, paintings, *Krugerrands*,
stamps, coins, cigarette cards, and almost anything else
which is collectable. These became fashionable investments
in the 1970s, when *Inflation* took off and shares were
unable to keep pace. But none of these alternatives offered
any income, so the money was tied up until the item was
sold. And, as with any fashion, the popularity of individual
items rose and fell without warning.

American Depository Receipt
This is a receipt issued by a US bank to show that the holder
owns a number of stocks or shares. It has been used to
enable investors to buy British shares without paying UK
Stamp duty.

Amortisation
The key part of this word is mort, from the French for

death. In business, if you amortise a debt or an asset, you kill
it financially. The debt is paid or the asset is regarded as
worthless, even if it is still chugging along.

Angel

A financial angel invests money in theatrical productions. If
the show is successful enough to cover its costs, profits are
then split between the angels and the management. A
common share-out is 60/40, but it can vary. Angels can
also be liable to put up overcall – extra money – if the show
turns out to be more expensive than first thought. It is
very risky, can be great fun, but do get a solicitor to comb
the contract before you sign.

Anna

The old unit of currency in India before decimalisation,
worth one-sixteenth of a rupee.

Annual General Meeting

Every company must hold an AGM at least once in each
calendar year, with a gap of not more than 15 months
between them. Shareholders are entitled to at least 21 days'
notice of the meeting, and they are normally sent a copy
of the latest annual report and accounts at the same time.
Legally, the meeting has to approve the dividend, elect
directors and agree to the auditors' fees. It is normally asked
to adopt the accounts. From time to time special
resolutions are proposed, to increase the directors' pay or
the number of shares in issue, or executive share incentive
schemes. Although most resolutions come from the board,
shareholders can make their own proposals. But check the
rules with the company secretary well in advance. See
Memorandum of association and *Articles of association*.

Annual percentage rate

Lenders advertising loans must tell what the interest charge
is going to work out at, under a legally-defined formula called
the APR. It is similar to what is known as the 'true' rate, as

opposed to the much lower 'flat' rate which tends to be publicised in instalment loans. See *True rate*, *Flat rate*.

Annuity
An annuity works in the opposite way to a *Life insurance* policy. Instead of paying a regular sum to collect a nest-egg at the end, for an annuity you present a nest-egg and receive a fixed income for the rest of your life. How much you get depends on current interest rates and how long you are likely to live. The younger you are, the smaller your monthly cheque. Inflation has made annuities a bad bet for all but very senior citizens.

Appropriation
This is a legalistic word for earmarking an asset for some future use. It may be a slice of land to be the site of a factory, or the money to build the factory. Sometimes organisations set up appropriation funds to collect money for a project.

Appropriation account
This is the account of a limited company which shows how the net profit for a period has been allocated. The credit side will show the balance brought down from the previous period, and the profit or loss which has just been recorded. The debit side will show that some has gone to pay dividends, some perhaps to reduce *Goodwill*, some to a specific reserve fund to pay for new machinery, say, and some to a general reserve. A small amount may be left over to carry forward.

APR See *Annual percentage rate*.

Arbitrage
Trading between different markets, often in different countries, to take advantage of price anomalies. While everyone in the London Stock Exchange may know the price of shares in Unilever, they may not be aware that the value of the Dutch guilder has shifted to make it cheaper to buy Unilever shares in Amsterdam. The same can happen in

gold, where London quotes a *Bullion* price in sterling while the rest of the world tends to quote bullion in US dollars.

Ariel
This is an alternative to the Stock Exchange. It started as an early attempt to introduce electronic share dealing, saving much of the commission charged by stockbrokers for dealing on the stock market proper. Its future is in doubt, now that fixed commissions are being scrapped in the Stock Exchange. Ariel's name stems from Automated Real-Time Investment Exchange Ltd.

Articles of association
The shareholders of each company must approve a set of articles of association when it is formed – and they must be allowed to vote on any proposed changes. The articles cover the internal rules of how the company is to be run: how many directors, their pay, how many authorised shares, borrowing limits, conditions for calling shareholders' meetings, rules for share transfers.

Assembled land
When developers move in on a block of land, they often have to buy it piecemeal, in small parcels. If they are successful, the resulting block, often an island site, can be developed in a coherent way after discussion with the local authority and, possibly, the Department of the Environment. However, assembled land makes complications when it comes to calculating *Development land tax*.

Assessment See *Notice of assessment*.

Asset
This can be anything useful that you own, even if you have borrowed the money to pay for it. Current assets are cash or close to it, like money owed by customers or stocks of goods for sale. Fixed assets are buildings, equipment (even cars) and investments in other businesses. Though they all sound

straightforward, arguments can rage about the true value of assets. How many customers will vanish or go bust before paying you? How much of your stock is out of date? What price would your equipment fetch if you had to sell or replace it?

Asset stripping
It is possible to buy the shares of many companies quoted on the Stock Exchange for less than the value of the assets the companies own. This is because they are not making enough profit or paying enough dividend. In the 1960s Jim Slater and others realised they could take over such companies and sell the assets piecemeal, leaving a tidy profit. But this often meant throwing more people out of work, and was sharply criticised.

Associate of a participator
In deciding who controls a *Close company*, certain people are counted as being associates of a *Participator*. They include spouse, parent, children, brother or sister, business partner, and a trustee of any settlement settled by the participator.

Association of British Chambers of Commerce
A business pressure group dating back to 1860. The Association, based at Sovereign House, 212–224 Shaftesbury Avenue, London WC2H 8EB, is the forum for a national network of 87 Chambers representing 50,000 businesses. It lobbies the government on economic, business and tax matters. The Association is a member of the Europe-wide Conférence Permanente des Chambres de Commerce et d'Industrie de la Communauté Economique Européenne.

Association of British Insurers
The organisation that represents most of the main insurance companies in the country. It is a source of information about the industry, and also looks into complaints about its members from members of the public. Even if you are not

insured with one of its members, it can probably give you some advice on where to take complaints about non-members. Under the ABI's wing is the *Life Offices Association*, which deals specifically with the life-insurance industry. Both are based at Aldermary House, Queen Street, London EC4N 1TT.

Association of Licensed Dealers in Securities *See National Association of Securities Dealers and Investment Managers.*

Assurance
This word is used by the insurance industry in regard to life policies. The reason is that death, unlike other things that can be insured, is a certainty. Surviving relatives are at least assured of some money. But in fact it is only another form of *Insurance*, often with an investment element added. See *Life insurance*.

Assured tenancy
This concept was introduced by the 1980 Housing Act. It applies only to newly built homes, and to encourage would-be landlords the tenancy is not protected or regulated, and the landlord can charge any rent. See *Fair rent, Regulated tenancy, Shorthold tenancy, Tenant.*

At best
A Stock Exchange term instructing a stockbroker to get the best price he can to buy or sell. It is used when prices are moving quickly and the investor does not want to tie the broker down to a particular price.

Attendance allowance
If you are in need of constant attention because of a mental or physical handicap, you may qualify for an attendance allowance to help pay for it. Your doctor should be able to tell you whether you qualify, but see also *Disability benefit*.

Auction
Taken from the Latin *auctionem*, a sale by increasing bids.
Most of the *Consumer laws* in this country are waived for
auctions, although a bent auctioneer can be prosecuted for
deception, or for misrepresentation if what you buy turns
out to be a fake. It is worth observing auctions a while before
taking part, to get the feel. And ask for a copy of the house
rules: these can vary, and ignorance may be costly. In
Scotland and the north of England an auction is sometimes
called a *Roup*.

Auditor
An accountant who audits a firm's accounts. If he is satisfied
he issues a certificate saying that the accounts give a 'true and
fair' view of the position on the balance-sheet date. If not,
he may withhold a certificate until he has enough
information or he may state his misgivings in the certificate.
The term 'auditor' comes from the time when the auditor
listened to the explanations of the company's officers.
Nowadays it is a question of examining documents,
including computer tapes, physically cross-checking a
sample of the assets, and much else.

Austral
Currency of Argentina. It is worth about 80p (at time of
writing).

Authorised capital
This is a legal and accounting term for the maximum
amount of money a company is allowed to raise by selling
shares. It is agreed by the shareholders, but cannot be less
than £2. This power forces the directors to go to the
shareholders whenever they want to increase the
figure – and shareholders are then very properly entitled
to ask them why. It is a gentle restraint on directors'
wilder expansion fantasies. Sometimes called nominal
capital.

AVC See *Additional voluntary contributions*.

Averaging See *Pound-cost averaging*.

AVMA See *Action for the Victims of Medical Accidents*.

Avoidance of tax
This is the legal attempt to cut your tax bill by taking advantages of quirks in the law – or, depending on your point of view, by conforming to the law's requirements. However, in recent years the Inland Revenue has cracked down on investment and other schemes whose sole object is tax avoidance. But it is still a lot less serious than *Evasion of tax*.

Avos See *Pataca*.

Back duty
If you forget or deliberately decide not to disclose certain sources of income, you will be liable to back duty. This can happen if you do a spare-time job or receive some interest or dividends which you overlook when you fill in your *Tax return*. The Inland Revenue will assess you for the arrears. They are allowed to accept a settlement instead of taking you to court.

Backwardation
This gives a stock market bear the chance to escape from a trap. If you have promised to sell shares you do not actually own, and the price then goes up instead of down, you will lose money if you deliver those shares on time. By paying a backwardation fee you can put the whole painful business off until the end of the next Stock Exchange Account.

Bad debt
A bad debt often begins as a matter of opinion, when a doubt forms whether a certain customer is going to pay. He may just be late, or you may have stronger evidence –

perhaps his phone has been cut. It is then a question of chasing. You may fail, in which case a moment arrives when the debt has to be written off as wholly bad. Or you may catch the debtor, it may have been a misunderstanding, or you may get some money back through the courts.

Baht
The main currency unit of Thailand in south-east Asia, worth about 40 to the pound. It is divided into 100 satang. Thailand has 25- and 50-satang coins, one- and five-baht coins, and notes in 10, 20 and 100 baht.

Balance of payments
Quite simply, this is the difference between the money a country pays and receives. It is divided into two parts. The first is called the current account, and measures imports and exports of goods – known as visibles – and services, such as tourism or insurance – referred to as invisibles. The second part is the capital account, covering flows of investment in and out of the country. The surplus from all these movements over the years is held in the form of reserves of gold bullion and foreign currency.

Balance sheet
A snapshot of a company's financial position at its year-end. Traditionally, the assets are on the right and the liabilities on the left or, as some absent-minded accountants prefer, 'nearest the window'. However, current liabilities can be lumped together with current assets to produce a net current asset figure – by deducting one from the other. The apparent magic is that a balance sheet always balances, but this is because every pound that is received automatically appears on both sides of the sheet. Any cash shown under assets is also a liability to shareholders or creditors. What to watch out for are the proportions – if loans swamp shareholders' funds, for example.

Balancing allowance/charge
When an asset is sold, the price is compared with the

written-down value for tax purposes. If it fetches less than
that, a balancing allowance can be set against the profits of
the business. But if the asset fetches more, there is a balancing
charge.

Balboa
The currency of Panama. Because of the United States' close
involvement in Panama, the balboa is tied to the dollar's
rate against other foreign currencies.

Baltic Exchange
Officially known as the Baltic Mercantile and Shipping
Exchange, this is the City of London's main shipping market
and also deals in commodities like grain and soya beans.
Like Lloyd's insurance market and the Stock Exchange,
the Baltic Exchange began in a coffee house in the eighteenth
century. Originally it specialised in putting ships and
cargoes together for voyages to and from the Baltic Seas.
Now it deals world-wide. Further details from the Baltic's
offices at 14–20, St Mary Axe, London EC3A 8BU.

Bank
A bank is a company whose main business is handling money
and providing finance. Under the *Banking Act 1979* banks
are divided into two main types: *recognised banks* and *licensed
deposit-takers*. A recognised bank is expected to provide the
full range of services – taking deposits, issuing cheques,
offering loans, providing a safe-deposit for valuables,
exchanging foreign currencies, discounting bills of exchange
and providing legal and trustee services.

Bank cash book
This is used by a business which wants to cut down the
amount of cash in employees' hands. Apart from petty cash,
every note and coin goes into the bank each night. This
book replaces the *Three-column cash book*. The idea behind
it is that it makes it easier to spot wrinkles in the trends –
and immediately investigate.

Bank Giro
The modern name for banks' credit transfers. It has nothing
to do with the State-owned *Girobank*, but is a cheaper way
of paying bills. Instead of writing a cheque for each bill, and
possibly sending them individually through the post, you
can collect several together, list them on a Bank Giro form
and pay for them with one cheque. But you do have to
take or send them to your own bank branch.

Bank of England
Britain's central bank. It is responsible for handling the
government's income and payments, as well as the issue of
notes and coins. It is the banker to the other banks and
executes the government's monetary policy, including
credit and rates of interest. The Bank also deals with foreign
central banks and with Britain's reserves of gold and
foreign exchange. Founded in 1694, it was nationalised in
1946. See *Lender of last resort*.

Bank rate
This was a rate set by the Bank of England as part of its
technique to manage the *Money market*. It was a penal rate
which *Discount* houses had to pay if they ran short of cash.
The result was that all other interest rates were tied to Bank
rate, so the Bank could adjust it whenever the government
wanted to make credit easier or tighter. Bank rate ceased
to be used in 1981.

Bank reconciliation statement
While the bank account in a firm's cash book runs closely
parallel with its account at the local bank, differences can
occur. A supplier may be slow in presenting a cheque, or it
may arrive too late to appear in the bank's latest statement.
The bank may receive credits for us, like a dividend, before
we know about them – and every so often it slips in its
own charges to us. So a bookkeeper's job is to reconcile the
two sets of figures and make them agree.

Bank statement
The scoreboard of your bank account. Banks vary as to how
often they will automatically send you one, but if you ask
they will normally agree to the frequency that suits you.
Once a month is enough for most people. Some of the
more exclusive banks, like the National Westminster
subsidiary Coutts, still stick to the admirable habit of
handwritten statements. But mostly it is a computer printout
showing the date, the number of the cheque or the name
of a *Standing order*, the amount in or out, and the cumulative
total – plus or minus. Ask very nicely and you might get a
smart folder to collect your statements in.

Bankers' Automated Clearing Services
A backroom scheme operated jointly by the London clearing
banks. Much of their cheque-clearing information is on
computer to save the cumbersome transfer of paper. BACS
coordinates this at the end of each day's business by
making the information available to each of the banks.

Banker's draft
In effect, a cheque drawn by a bank branch on its head
office. It guarantees immediate payment, and is used where
the parties to a deal need to know that the money will be
transferred within a certain time.

Banking Act 1979
This Act set up a framework for the Bank of England to
supervise banks and other organisations which take deposits
from the public. It was framed in the wake of the secondary
banking crisis of 1974, and does not cover *Building societies*
and *Trustee savings banks* as they were already under control.
See *Deposit protection scheme*, *Licensed deposit-taker*, *Recognised
bank*.

Banking Information Service
Set up by the *Committee of London Clearing Banks*, BIS can
give general information about banks, and has access to a

formidable mass of statistics on the subject. May not be able
to answer individual queries, but should know where to
refer you. Address is 10 Lombard Street, London EC3V
9AP.

Banknote
A piece of paper issued by a government for use as *Money*.
It is printed with its face value and a series of patterns
designed to make it both recognisable and difficult to forge.
Banknotes had their origin in notes written by goldsmiths,
and then banks as receipts for gold deposited with them. In
Britain, one or two Scottish banks are still allowed to print
their own notes, but the quantity is strictly regulated by the
State.

Bankrupt
A bankrupt is someone whose property is managed under
the Bankruptcy Acts for the benefit of his or her creditors.
It is also the adjective describing a bankrupt. A person
becomes bankrupt when he or she is unable to pay debts
and is taken to court by the creditors. Only people become
bankrupt. Companies go into liquidation or receivership.

Bargain
An ancient word meaning to haggle or negotiate – and the
result of that haggling. When people think they have bought
cheaply, they say they have got a bargain. But on the Stock
Exchange, every time a stock or share changes hands, the
deal is called a bargain.

Barter
A system of exchange which operated before money became
acceptable, and can still be used today by traders who
want to avoid the use of money. Prices of goods or services
are struck between buyer and seller in terms of other goods
or services: if you mow my lawn I'll give you a bottle of
whisky. The trouble is that every buyer automatically
becomes a seller, and vice versa. What happens if no one

wants what you are willing to offer? It is much less flexible than money, but attempts have been made to set up modern barter systems, mainly to avoid tax.

Base rate
The basis of each bank's structure of interest rates. The term was introduced in 1971 when banks were encouraged to compete. So closely do they compete, however, that none dare stay out of line for long: money would simply flood in or out. The interest a bank pays on deposit accounts tends to be about 2 per cent below the base rate, while it charges borrowers from 1 to 5 per cent over base.

Basic component
This is the bedrock of the government pension scheme, introduced in its present form at 5s (25p) a week in 1948. In 1961 it was supplemented by an *Earnings related pension*, and from 1975 increases were tied to the *Retail prices index*, the main indicator of *Inflation*. If both husband and wife have made regular *National Insurance* contributions, each receives a single person's pension, but if one of them has not worked regularly the former breadwinner collects a married couples' pension. See *Additional component, Pension, State pension*.

Basic rate tax See *Income tax*.

Basis
The difference between the cash value of a *Financial instrument* and the price of a *Futures contract* in that instrument. See *Basis point, London International Financial Futures Exchange*.

Basis point
A movement of 0.01% in the price of a *Futures contract*. This is also known as a minimum price fluctuation, point or tick.

Bear
A pessimist on the stock market, who is trying to claw down

the prices of stocks and shares. He expects prices to go
down, possibly because he thinks bad news is about to come
out. If he has any shares which he thinks will fall, he will
sell them, hoping to buy at a lower price. A bear speculator
will sell shares he does not own, with the intention of
buying more cheaply before he has to deliver the original
parcel. Stock Exchange rules give him up to three weeks
to do this. But if a lot of bears are playing the same game,
the jobbers who make the market will anticipate them by
pushing the price back up again. This is called a bear squeeze
and can be very painful on the pocket.

Bearer shares
These are shares in companies which do not keep a register
of shareholders. So the shares are like banknotes: they are
your only proof of ownership. British companies are
required by law to keep a share register.

Beneficiary
Someone who gains from someone else doing them a good
turn. It is often used nowadays to refer to someone named
to receive a *Legacy* from a *Will*. See also *Tax deduction
certificate*.

Bequest
A Middle English word, possibly stemming from a word
meaning a saying or declaration, but now used to refer to
a gift made through a *Will*. See also *Legacy*.

Beta analysis
This is a statistical technique for predicting how share prices
are likely to move. A share that moves exactly in step with
the market as a whole has a beta rating of one. If it rises and
falls faster than the market, it scores more than one:
slower, and its rating is less than one. The idea is to get on
to high-beta shares if you think the market is due for a
boom, but switch to the low betas on the downturn. Easier
said than done. See also *Z-score*.

Betting profits

People who make their living from betting can be in a
difficult tax position. If you bet on horses from home and
stick to starting prices, the Inland Revenue does not reckon
you have to pay Income Tax. But you do have to pay
Income Tax if you live from betting regularly at race
meetings: that is called a vocation as far as the taxman is
concerned.

Bid

Stock, share and unit trust prices are also *Quoted* in pairs –
Bid and *Offer*. The bid is the price at which the market
will buy from you. Sadly, it is always the lower of the two.
A bid can also refer to a *Takeover* offer.

Bill

From the Latin, *bulla*, meaning a seal. It subsequently came
to refer to a document with a seal on it, making it formal
or official. This meaning is still used for parliamentary Bills,
which propose new laws: if passed, they become Acts. In
financial terms, a bill is a document which lists goods or
services supplied and due for payment. See also *Lading*.

Billion

There is a lot of confusion about billions, because Britain
worked on the basis of a billion which was bigger than was
used in the United States. However, the American billion –
equal to a thousand million, or 1,000,000,000 – has taken
over to the extent that it is now the measure used by the
UK Treasury, and all British newspapers have followed
suit. The British version was a million million. See *Trillion*.

Bill of exchange

When goods are traded, the buyer usually asks for time to
pay so that he in turn has time to sell them on. The bill
of exchange, or commercial bill, is an IOU or promise to
pay on an agreed future date. But the seller may not want
to wait that time. What he can do is to take the bill to an

Accepting house. If the accepting house is confident that
the debtor will pay up, he accepts the bill, at a *Discount*
equal to the going rate of interest. The better the risk, the
lower the discount. The best are called fine trade bills, and
have a discount rate nearly as low as that on *Treasury bills*.

Birr
Ethiopia's currency, worth about 30p.

Black market
An unofficial market which springs up to break the official
rules, usually in times of scarcity. When goods are in short
supply, the government tries to ensure an even spread by
rationing. The black marketeer exists to supply buyers
who want more than their ration and are willing to pay over
the odds to get it. Diverting supplies of butter and eggs
to the black market in wartime causes misery, but the only
way to kill the practice is to raise the official price, as in
the case of Cup Final tickets.

Blind person's allowance
This is a tax allowance for anyone who is registered as blind
with their local authority. The yardstick is that the eyesight
must be so poor that the sufferer cannot do any job which
normally requires vision. It is not paid as a lump sum.
Instead the blind person is allowed to keep a large slice of
income tax-free.

Block trading
This is a US term for trading in blocks of stocks or shares
far larger than the market can swallow in one go, worth
perhaps at least £250,000. The broker dealer may decide to
take the block onto its own book and take the risk of
finding buyers willing to pay higher prices.

Blue chip
A top-quality share – usually in a large, solid, dependable
and not very exciting company. The 30 shares which make

up the *Financial Times industrial ordinary index* all count as
blue chips. After that, it's a matter of opinion. The phrase
comes from America, where its origin lay in the colour of
the highest value of gambling chips.

Bolivar
Venezuela's currency, the bolivar is worth about 13p.

Bond washing
Since the 1985 Budget, any income built into the price of a
bond will be taxed as income if it is sold before the income
has been received.

Bonus
According to the *Shorter Oxford Dictionary*, this is a piece of
eighteenth-century Stock Exchange slang from the Latin
bonum, meaning good. Insurance companies pay it on your
policy when they have actually made the profits on their
investments you might have expected in the first place.
Employers, including stock market firms, pay it to some
workers as an incentive to work harder. This is nearer to
the dictionary definition: 'a boon or gift over and above
what is normally due'.

Book
A market maker keeps a book of his positions in the stocks
he trades, partly for record purposes and partly so that he
can easily see whether his overall position is *long* or *short* of
stock.

Book Entry Transfer
Because of the rising cost of issuing new certificates every
time a share changes hands, there has been pressure to allow
a system of book entry transfer, whereby the change of
ownership is effected simply by altering the share register.
But that has profound legal implications for the British laws
relating to contract and property. See *Bearer shares*, *share
certificate*.

Bookkeeping

This is the job of keeping records of a business's transactions, as raw materials and labour are paid for and money finally received for the finished goods or services. When the result of all these transactions is added up, what emerges is the *Balance sheet*. Bookkeeping is not to be confused with bookmaking, which has to do with shouting the odds on a bet.

Boom

The term for an economic or financial explosion – of the non-destructive sort. It describes the time when the economy as a whole, or a particular part of it, is expanding rapidly, with higher turnover, rising prices and more employment. There are varying grades of slowdown from a boom, including *Recession*, *Depression* and *Slump*, all of which are part of the *Trade cycle*.

Borrowing

'Neither a borrower nor a lender be,' says Polonius in *Hamlet*. But the truth is that industry would grind to a halt if there were no borrowing, and business relies on the public borrowing to buy much of the goods in the shops. But borrowing itself is like a street market: all the lenders are shouting their wares. In general, the quicker you want the money and the less security you can offer, the higher the interest rate you will be charged. It is well worth taking your time and shopping around.

Bought deal

A technique whereby a company announces its intention to raise money through an issue of securities and investment firms bid to buy the whole block of the securities. The firm offering the highest price then tries to distribute the securities through investment funds and other investors. It is a US device which many expect to become prevalent in Britain.

Bourse
The European name for a Stock Exchange, or money
market. It comes from the Latin word for a treasury,
which is also the origin of the English word bursary.

Box
A room of box-like proportions near the floor of the Stock
Exchange. It is used by broker/dealers to communicate with
their offices and take the weight off their legs.

Break
A sudden, sharp fall in a price on a financial market.

Break-up value See *Net asset value*.

Bretton Woods
A town in New Hampshire, United States, which in 1944
hosted a conference of nations to lay down an international
financial system for the world. Its two lasting legacies are
the *International Monetary Fund* and the *World Bank*. But
the actual system it spawned was formally ended by
President Nixon of the USA in 1971, when he announced that
gold and US dollars were no longer freely interchangeable.
This had been the lynchpin of the Bretton Woods
agreement, which relied on fairly fixed exchange rates among
the major currencies. The devaluation of the British pound
in 1967 foreshadowed the end of that. See *Keynes*,
Smithsonian Agreement.

Bridging loan
This is a loan designed to tide you over a temporary problem.
The classic reason for a bridging loan is if you are moving
house. You have bought your new place, but you can't
manage to unload your old home. Result: you have to keep
paying for both at once, to say nothing of the actual costs
of moving. Bank managers are understanding about this
sort of case, because they can normally see that it should
sort itself out within a few months. The golden rule from

the would-be borrower's point of view is to explain the
situation at the earliest opportunity. Then he can advise
you, and may even know some of the other people involved.

British Association for Counselling
This is a charity paid for by companies. It offers to put
people in touch with local *Counselling* services. This itself
costs individuals nothing, but the services themselves may
do. The association's address is 37a Sheep Street, Rugby,
Warwickshire CV21 3BX.

British Franchise Association
A body which aims to maintain standards in the *Franchise*
industry. Members are franchising firms, which must have
been trading for at least three years and have at least three
franchisees, all of whom are checked with credit-rating
agencies. The BFA's ambition is to prevent a repetition of
the *Pyramid-selling* businesses which gave franchising a
bad name in the 1970s. Its address is 75a Bell Street,
Henley-on-Thames, Oxon RG9 2BD.

British Insurance Brokers' Association
This is the association which speaks for insurance brokers.
It is not a statutory body, but most of the reputable brokers
belong to it and it can give you advice about any problems
you may have. Its address is BIBA House, 14 Bevis Marks,
London EC3A 7NT. See also *Insurance Brokers' Registration
Council*.

British Standards Institution
The BSI's kitemark seal of approval has become famous as
a sign that the goods in question have been properly made.
Financed by government grant and publishing sales, BSI is
non-profit-making and has set standards for several
thousand products. Most are industrial, but there is also a
wide range of consumer goods. The BSI is at 2 Park Street,
London W1Y 2BS. See also *Consumer law*.

British Technology Group
The latest version of a holding company for the government's
investments in industry. The modern series began in 1967
with the Industrial Reorganisation Corporation. That was
scrapped by the Heath government, but recreated by
Wilson as the National Enterprise Board under the 1975
Industry Act. The NEB's powers were cut by Thatcher, but
it was given more purpose by being merged with the National
Research and Development Corporation to form the
British Technology Group. This holds long-standing
investments in such companies as BL and Rolls-Royce, and
is also the vehicle for encouraging new industries like the
microchip.

Brokerage
The money received by a broker in return for his services.
It is synonymous with *Commission*.

Broker dealer
The form that stockbroking firms are taking under the new
Stock Exchange rules. Most of them will continue to act
purely as brokers, as they always did. But under the new
rules they are also allowed to act as a dealer in securities
in their own right. They must deal with a market maker on
behalf of clients, unless they can offer a better deal off
their own book. This can be verified by time-stamping.

Budget
The annual occasion for the Chancellor of the Exchequer to
review the economic situation and 'propose' remedies. If the
Chancellor's party has a majority in Parliament, the
proposals tend to go through, and they have had a reputation
of bringing bad news to individuals as governments have
taken a bigger share of national income for their own
spending plans – and then kept raising taxes to combat
inflation. In 1947 Chancellor Dalton resigned after leaking a
tiny part of his Budget before the big moment. But recently
the Budget's main options have been widely discussed,

and the importance of the traditional March or April
set-piece has been devalued by a habit of supplementing it
with a number of *'Mini-Budgets'*. See also *Tax, Finance Act*.

Budget accounts
These come in two quite distinct varieties. One is the sort
you can get from a store, and is a form of *Charge account*.
The other is an arrangement you can have with your bank.
Here you say you will put so much a month into the
account and the bank agrees to pay off your household bills.
That way you avoid the horrible peaks when all the bills
seem to come in at once, in the winter and at holiday time.

Building society
It is called a society because the first ones were little more
than clubs, and it is a building society because those clubs got
together to build a house for each of their members. When
they all had a roof over their heads, the society was wound
up. Now, though, they are vast machines for savings and
Mortgages. If you are thinking of buying a house, your
first step should be to open a savings account with a building
society, to show you can put some money by. As with any
financial organisation you come across, it is also worth
making personal contact. Most of the societies are
represented by the Building Societies Association, 3 Savile
Row, London W1X 1AF. See *Ordinary share account,
Subscription share account, Term shares, Escalator share,
Insurance-linked building society savings*.

Bull
One of the three species in the stock market menagerie, the
others being *Bears* and *Stags*. A bull is someone who
expects the price of a particular stock or share, or even the
market as a whole, to go up. So he buys now, hoping that
enough other investors will follow him to drive the price up.
When he thinks the price is as high as it is likely to go, he
intends to sell. In practice, this can be the hardest decision
of all. The bull who really wants to speculate will order

shares without paying for them, relying on the Stock
Exchange account system to give him up to three weeks to
find the money. He is trusting that he can sell by then, pay
the original cost and pocket the difference. Easier said
than done. A bull who becomes uncertain is called, and
usually smells, stale.

Bulldog bond
Nickname for a bond used by a foreign government agency
to borrow money in London. Bulldog bonds are
denominated in sterling and carry a fixed rate of interest.
Although they normally pay a higher rate of interest than
a British Gilt-edged stock (see *Gilts*), they are often traded
as gilts. London is attractive to foreign borrowers because of
the UK's blend of relatively high interest rates and tax
incentives. If, in addition, sterling is strong new bulldogs
begin to appear. Similar foreign bonds raised in New York
are called Yankees, and the Tokyo equivalent is known as
a Samurai bond.

Bullion
An ancient English word for gold or silver, in ingot or coins.
It is used in talking about the metal itself in its purest form.

Business
In its original form, busyness was simply any activity that
kept you busy. But since the time when the 'y' was dropped
in favour of the 'i' around about 1600, it has become more
and more closely connected with the world of *Commerce*,
as any work aimed at making a *Profit*. A business became
an entity in itself, and eventually businesses were given
separate legal status from individuals. Since 1965 they have
had their own fully-fledged tax system, although there was
a crude profits tax before that.

Business entertaining
Buying a meal for a trade contact cannot be set against
profits unless the guest is foreign. In any case, the

entertainment must be 'of a kind and on a scale' which the Inland Revenue considers reasonable. Anything which is given in the ordinary course of trade is allowable against tax, as is any small gift, so long as it is not food, drink, tobacco or a voucher for goods. Entertainment between employees of the same firm does not count as business entertaining, but it still has to be reasonable.

Business Expansion Scheme

Announced in the 1983 Budget as the successor to the Business Start-up Scheme. It gives tax relief to people who buy shares in genuine trading companies, so long as they are not quoted on the Stock Exchange or the Unlisted Securities Market. Investors must put in at least £500 in any one year, they must not be controlling shareholders, directors or employees of the business, and the money must be left in for at least five years. Financial and other companies do not qualify. Do get professional advice before committing yourself. Research and development firms now included.

Business Start-up Scheme

Introduced in the 1981 Finance Act, this scheme was intended to use tax reliefs to encourage people to invest in new UK businesses. The investors could not be connected with the venture in any other way, and must leave their money in for at least five years. The Inland Revenue decided which businesses qualified. See *Business Expansion Scheme*.

Buy

An Old English word of unknown origin, it means to acquire something in return for an agreed sum of money. Until recently, British law gave remarkably little protection to a buyer after he had bought. But consumerism is beginning to change that. See *Office of Fair Trading*, *Purchase*, *Sell*.

Buy back

A phrase ushered in by the 1982 Finance Act to refer to

cases where a company buys back its own shares.
Previously this was ruled out by the fact that the money
paid by the company was treated as equal to a dividend,
and taxed accordingly. The Inland Revenue can now waive
such tax if a series of conditions is fulfilled. The deal must
not be aimed principally at avoiding tax, and the shares must
be sold by a UK resident who has held them for normally
at least five years. The deal must benefit the company's
trade, which must not be in share-dealing, land, securities
or *futures*.

Buy on close
At the end of a trading session on a financial market,
securities are quoted at the closing *Bid* and *Offer* prices for
the day. Anyone who buys on close has got a price within
the two closing levels. The same thing at the start of the
day is called buy on opening.

Call
A call can be any demand for money. A loan that has to be
repaid on demand is known as money at call or call money.
The instalments on *Partly-paid* stocks and shares are also
termed calls.

Capacity
The most that a firm can produce from the amount of land,
factory space, machinery and labour that it has the use of,
not forgetting the management's ingenuity. It has also been
adopted by the *Insurance* industry to indicate how much
risk an insurer can take on.

Capital
Any money that is used in a business or, as the economist
Adam Smith put it, to produce a revenue. Between them,
the economists and the accountants have come up with
dozens of types and definitions, from 'auxiliary capital' for
equipment to 'natural capital' for land.

Capital account
Part of the *Balance of payments*, showing the movement of
investment money in and out of the country. It can be a
confusing set of figures to interpret. An outflow of capital
cuts the reserves of foreign currency and can depress the
exchange rate, but it should eventually produce a stream of
dividends back into the country. Those dividends will
appear in the *Current account*. For bookkeeping definition,
see *Personal account*.

Capital allowance
Some types of spending on capital for a business are allowed
against tax. This means that such spending can be deducted
from profits before tax is assessed on those profits. Under
the Capital Allowances Act 1968, the approved spending
categories are: plant and machinery, industrial or
agricultural buildings and agricultural land, mines, oil wells,
dredging, and capital spending on scientific research. See
*Balancing allowance, First-year allowance, Initial
allowance, Writing-down allowance*.

Capital employed
This broadly is the same as the liabilities side of the *Balance
sheet*. It shows how much money is in the business, and where
it has come from. The assets part of the balance sheet shows
how that money has been used.

Capital Gains Tax
Introduced by James Callaghan in 1965, CGT takes 30% of
any profits you make from buying and selling investments,
after allowing for inflation. The first £6,300 of gains in any
one year go free. The investments can range from shares
to houses and include paintings and jewellery. Happily,
though, there are plenty of exemptions. Cars and houses
do not count, unless the Inland Revenue decide that you are
making a living by trading in them. Other exemptions are
profits on life insurance policies, gambling winnings, gains
on UK government stock and corporate bonds. However,

if in doubt take professional advice, as the inflation
allowances are complex. See *Gross fund*.

Capital Tax
A capital tax is a tax on people's capital, or wealth. The
tradition in Britain has been to levy such taxes at the moment
when the wealth is transferred. The first attempt in modern
times was estate duty, which taxed the estate of a dead
person before it was handed round to the inheritors. But
this was effectively replaced by *Capital Transfer Tax*.
Another tax opportunity was created with the invention of
Capital Gains Tax, taken at the point when an asset is sold
for profit. The fullest version of a capital tax is the *Wealth
tax*, which has been much debated but by 1986 not yet
introduced.

Capital Transfer Tax See *Inheritance Tax*.

Capitalisation issue See *Scrip issue*.

Carat
A measure of the weight of precious stones and the purity
of gold. Diamonds were once measured against the fruit
of the carob, an evergreen Mediterranean tree. The carat
has since 1932 been defined as 200 milligrams. For reasons
which are not clear, pure gold was defined as containing 24
carats. A one-carat lump of metal is 1/24th gold, 12-carat
is half gold and so on.

Careers and Occupational Information Centre
A branch of the *Manpower Services Commission*, publishing
what it calls a series of audio-visual teaching packs for sale to
schools and colleges. COIC also produces a large amount of
free material. Ask the MSC for more details at Moorfoot,
Sheffield S1 4PQ.

Carry
The cost of carrying on a *Position* in a *Financial instrument*.

Cartel
When the word was coined in the sixteenth century, a cartel was a letter of defiance. The defiance remains in its business context as a group of firms which stay separate, but agree on prices, output and marketing. It is a bid to reach out for the advantages of a monopoly, and can be the tool of an *Oligopoly*. The first cartels appeared in Germany, and there were notorious examples in the sugar and rubber trades in the 1920s and 1930s. The best present-day example is the Central Selling Organisation for diamonds operated by De Beers.

Cash
Cash is ready *Money* in the form of coins and notes.

Cash and new
If you want to hold shares over from one Stock Exchange account to another, you can sell them free of commission at the end of one account, and immediately buy them again for the next account. It puts off the moment of actually having to pay for the shares. A small charge is levied though.

Cash basis
Some businesses are run on a cash basis, whereby income is credited only when it has been received. Spending may be charged in the normal way. This method is used by professional people such as doctors and barristers because they cannot sue for fees.

Cash cow
A slick piece of jargon for a business which may not make much profit, but generates plenty of cash. Just as a real cow is milked for an ulterior purpose – to feed humans – so the financial version is usually 'milked' so that the money can be used elsewhere. Some large groups of companies own supermarkets for that reason. The food suppliers give them perhaps three months to pay for goods which the public will pay for almost immediately. See *Cash pig*.

Cash discount See *Settlement discount*.

Cash flow
A weapon of financial management. It is measured by adding
depreciation, any deferred tax provision and net attributable
profits. This is the total money generated by trade for
reinvestment in the business. The cash flow can be rated
against previous performance, and against the cash needs of
the company. These are for new assets and working capital,
and if they top cash flow for too long the company will have
to raise cash elsewhere, by borrowing or making a share
issue. The sums are often done for you in the annual
accounts, in what is called the 'Statement of source and
application of funds'.

Cashing in insurance See *Surrender*.

Cash pig
The financial opposite of a *Cash cow*. It is a business
operation which eats up money. If the whole of a business did
this, it would very soon go bust, but most companies have
to put up with at least a part of their organisation spending
the money rather than earning it. Every firm needs to devote
some time – and therefore money – to personnel,
administration, form-filling, and the like. In grander outfits
this is known as the head office function. Some types of
business cannot help feeding other cash pigs. Most
manufacturers spend some resources on research and
development. It can be all too easy for R & D to get out of
hand.

Caveat emptor
A Latin phrase meaning 'let the buyer beware'. For a long
time it was the basis of English consumer law. It was up
to the buyer to make sure that he was getting what he
wanted, and that it was in the condition he wanted.
However, that has changed, thanks to the *Office of Fair
Trading* and an ever-lengthening list of *Consumer laws*.

CBI See *Confederation of British Industry*.

Cedi
Ghana's currency, worth around 2p.

Cent
Basis of the decimal currency system, which most countries adhere to since Britain abandoned pounds, shillings and pence in 1971. As its name implies, the cent is one-hundredth of its parent unit, such as the dollar. A near cousin is the franc's centime. But there are many alternative labels for the equivalents in other currencies: the UK sticks to 100 pennies to the pound.

Central bank
A bank which acts to execute a government's monetary manoeuvres and to regulate the money markets of an economy. It supervises interest rates, the issue of banknotes, and the government's borrowing needs. It is the lender of last resort in the financial market, making it effectively the other banks' bank. The central bank normally stores official holdings of gold and foreign currency, and controls the movement of foreign exchange in and out of the country.

Central Government Borrowing Requirement
This is the difference between the income received – mainly through taxes – and the money spent by the government departments in and around Whitehall. In analysing government economic policy, this figure is often contrasted with the wider *Public Sector Borrowing Requirement*.

Certificate of age exemption
Once you are old enough to claim the *State pension*, you no longer have to pay National Insurance contributions, whether or not you keep working. To qualify you must ask the Department of Health and Social Security for a certificate of age exemption, which you give to your employer so that he can stop making the deductions from your pay.

Certificate of deposit
This is a device to speed the flow of money round the City
of London. Companies, like individuals, often put spare cash
on deposit. To get the best rates of interest, they have to tie
the money up for a year or more. However, the bank that
takes the deposit gives the lender a certificate recording the
amount, length of time and rate of interest. Now if the
company wants to get at the money it can sell that certificate
on the money market – at a discount, of course.
Dollar-denominated CDs appeared in London in 1966, and
sterling CDs in 1968.

Certificate of tax deposit
This is a good wheeze for any well-off person who wants to
earn a good rate of interest on money he is going to hand over
to the taxman at some stage. The certificate is issued by the
Inland Revenue in minimum units of £2,000 and £500
thereafter, and you can simply use them to pay your tax bill
in the usual way – after paying income tax on the interest,
of course. You can cash them, but then the interest rate is
cut.

Chamber of Commerce See *Association of British Chambers
of Commerce*.

Charge accounts
'Charge it to my account, my good man!' says the dowager
duchess as she sweeps out of Harrods with a quarter-pound
of best cheddar. This is how many of us imagine charge
accounts, but like so much else they have been brought up to
date – and down to the reach of most shoppers. The
difference is that today's charge accounts expect the customer
to keep in close touch with the retailer. There are several
variations on the theme. Some operate just like a credit
card except that they are tied to a particular store chain.
With others, you agree to pay in so much a month and in
return you are allowed to spend up to 24 times that figure.
Of course, you pay interest on the difference between what

you have spent and what you have paid in so far. This is
sometimes called a budget account, and is a far cry from
what the duchess would be used to. The old-style charge
accounts, which are dying out, simply required the
customer to pay off the debt at the end of each month.
Interest might or might not be charged after that date –
depending how valued the customer was.

Charts
An attempt to turn share price movements into train
timetables. Chartists make graphs out of the trends in
market prices and, for that matter, share indices. They argue
that the type and volatility of the trend shows what the
market has been thinking about that share – and,
controversially, that from that you can predict what the market
is going to think. Like life and death, the second part of the
theory has never been proved, and most chartists are as
poor as you or I. The rich ones make money by selling
newsletters. But if the trend is distinct enough their advice
can be worth bearing in mind, as it may influence the
market's behaviour.

Chattel
An ancient word which may share roots with 'capital'. It
means simply all property except land and buildings. It used
to include money, too, but that meaning is now obsolete.

Check trading
The checks in question are vouchers which people can use
to buy goods. They are sold by *Finance houses*, who then send
representatives round the houses to collect instalment
payments on the checks – plus interest.

Cheque
A cheque tells a bank to pay a specified amount of money
to a specified person or organisation. Creditors can refuse
them, because they are not legal tender – so do not try
paying a bus fare with one. However, once accepted a

cheque can be a lot easier and more secure than cash. And it can be written on anything from a piece of paper to an egg. But banks do take a dim view of such gestures – and may load your charges accordingly.

Cheque card

A card issued by your bank so that you can prove to shopkeepers that your cheque will not bounce. They cost nothing, and the banks give them to all but their most unreliable or impoverished customers. They have become so widely accepted that they are well-nigh essential on any shopping trip beyond the local newsagents'. But they have two snags at present. One is that, because they give the retailer a guarantee that the cheque will go through, you cannot stop the cheque if you are unhappy with what you have bought. The other is that the card guarantees purchases up to only £50, which rules out most furniture and domestic appliances and more and more clothing. The reason for this is that the banks get nothing out of it except a growing list of fraud cases involving stolen cheque cards. They will die out as electronic systems move into the business of money transfer. See *Credit card*, *Debit card*.

Chief Registrar of Friendly Societies See *Friendly Societies*.

Child benefit

This is payable to anyone who is responsible for bringing up children. It applies to children up to 16, or 18 if they are studying up to GCE 'A' level or Ordinary National Diploma. It is not payable if the child is under a local authority, and there are complicated rules for children of parents from abroad or living abroad. Normally the mother collects the benefit, but it can be assigned to the father. Single parents can claim an extra sum called the child benefit increase. Ask your local social security office for details.

Children

Any money a child earns is taxed as though he or she were

an adult. They get the full *Single person's allowance* before
they have to pay any tax. This includes money given to them
by anyone but their parents. Mum and dad do, however,
rank for a *Child benefit* and may qualify for *Family income
supplement*, *Child's special allowance*, *Guardian's allowance*,
or *Additional personal allowance for children*. See *National
Children's Bureau*.

Child's special allowance
This is paid to a mother whose marriage has been dissolved
or annulled, and whose ex-husband has died. She must not
have remarried, her ex-husband must have been helping to
support the child, and she must be entitled to *Child benefit*.
It is tied to the father's national insurance contribution
record.

Chinese wall
A mythical concept. It refers to the separation of conflicting
departments within a financial firm, such as broking, fund
management and market-making, so that the conflicts are –
theoretically – avoided. Some of the bigger firms have
gone as far as putting different departments in different
buildings. But sceptics wondered how effective this
physical separation would be in practice.

Churning
A technique used by unscrupulous *Stockbrokers* to siphon
more commission from their clients' accounts. Where a
client has a *Discretionary account*, the broker can easily find
excuses to sell some of the shares in that *Portfolio* and buy
others instead. As brokers are in many cases paid commission
on each bargain they initiate, churning gives them two
extra payments, one for the sale and another for the
purchase. The broker hopes that this will be disguised by an
increase in the overall value of the portfolio, and that the
grateful client will not ask too many awkward questions
about the number of deals. But it does not always work out
as happily as that.

C.i.f.

Cost, Insurance, Freight. Anyone who buys goods c.i.f. is
getting them from abroad with the cost of insurance and
freight included in the price. If you think you can arrange
those extras cheaper yourself, you should buy *F.o.b.*

Citizens' Advice Bureau

This is an office where you can walk in off the street and
ask for free advice on almost anything – though it tends to
specialise in legal and money matters. It is run by a national
organisation, but is paid for by the local authorities as part
of their service to ratepayers. The advisers are mainly
volunteers. The address of your nearest branch will be in
the telephone book.

City

In the money world, the City means more than just a
densely-packed collection of streets and buildings. It refers
to the City of London, an ancient square mile which contains
every conceivable financial service. The *Bank of England*
is based there, as are the *Clearing banks'* head offices and
the leading financial markets, such as the *Stock Exchange*.
Many books have been written about the City, but you can
obtain free information from the Information Department,
Corporation of London, Guildhall, London EC2.

Claim

A demand for what you believe to be rightfully yours. If
you think you have a claim on an insurance policy, you should
ask the insurer for a claim form so that you can file the
necessary details.

Classical economics

This was the first attempt to codify economics. Ironically,
the late eighteenth-century thinkers behind it were trying
to argue the existence of a natural law that there were, in
effect, no economic laws – that governments could do little
about it, and free markets produced the best result. The

leading lights were Adam Smith, who wrote *An Inquiry into the Nature and Causes of the Wealth of Nations* in 1776, David Ricardo and T. R. Malthus. See *Subsistence theory of wages*.

Clawback
What the taxman giveth, the taxman also taketh away. Clawback occurs where taxpayers qualify for tax relief at one point, but are subsequently disqualified because of a change in their circumstances. Ironically, a clawback used to be the name for a toady or a crawler, on the notion of 'you scratch my back . . .'.

Clearing banks
These are the banks which form the clearing system for cheques and other money transfers. This happens in a London clearing house, where millions of slips of paper are swopped. At the end of the day they settle any net amounts owned by one bank to another. The clearing banks include the big four, Barclays, Lloyds, Midland and National Westminster, and the Royal Bank of Scotland.

Clearing member
A Stock Exchange firm which handles the paperwork for other firms. See *Introducing member*.

Clergymen
Men of the cloth get special tax treatment. They can set against tax a quarter of what they spend on rent, maintenance, repairs, insurance and managing their churches.

Close
The end of a trading session in a financial market. It can also refer to the closing price of an item on that market.

Close a position See *Position*.

Close company
The idea of a close company was invented as a way of

stopping attempts at *Avoidance of tax*. It is defined as a company which is either under the control of five or fewer *Participators*, or under the control of participators who are directors. Alternatively, if the company's income were to be divided up, more than half would go to the five ruling participators, or the participators who are directors. The details are in the Income and Corporation Taxes Act, 1970.

Coin
A piece of metal stamped with a recognisable pattern to show its origin and value, and used as *Money*. Nowadays invariably issued by governments, who threaten severe penalties for anyone who challenges their local monopoly. Originally coins were of gold and silver, and worth their face value, eliminating scope for forgery. Now cheaper alloys are used, and the coins are mere tokens relying for their value on scarcity and the willingness of people to accept them in payment. See *Banknote*.

Collateral
Collateral, so the old joke runs, is what you show your bank manager to prove you don't need the loan you are asking for. But if you have got it, it certainly should make that loan cheaper. It is really another word for security and literally means something that runs alongside your loan. Stocks and shares, the deeds of your house (if you have paid off your mortgage), even valuables such as stamps, jewellery or paintings can act as collateral. But don't be too optimistic. Your bank manager will put a much lower value on such assets than they would fetch on the market, to give him some cushion against their value suddenly dropping.

Collectors of Taxes
A self-explanatory title for the civil servants who are responsible for collecting the tax which *Inspectors of Taxes* have decided individuals should pay. See *Commissioners of Inland Revenue*.

Colón
The currency unit of two Central American republics, Costa
Rica and El Salvador. The Costa Rican colón is officially rated
at 36 to the pound, but at the 'free' rate it changes hands at
62 to the pound. In El Salvador, a colón is worth about
20p.

Columnar bookkeeping
If a businessman wants to analyse his trading closely, perhaps
to see how individual departments compare, the answer is
divide the main accounts book into columns. It is easier in
this way to see if one type of cost is getting out of hand,
or if an individual department's sales are slipping. See
Bookkeeping, Cross-tot.

Comecon
In full, the Council for Mutual Economic Assistance. It is
the economic part of the Warsaw Pact, which binds the
countries of eastern Europe to the USSR. Cuba and
Mongolia are also members.

Commerce
The word that stresses the trading and exchange side of
Business, as opposed to *Manufacture* or *Industry*. First used
in this country in 1537, it literally refers to the bringing
together of merchandise. It was once a verb as well as a
noun, but the verb fell into disuse, robbing us of the word
'commercer', to describe a *Merchant* or *Tradesman*.

Commercial bills See *Bills of exchange.*

Commission
Originally an authority to act for someone in an agreed
activity, from the idea of committing someone. But in the
mercenary days of the early eighteenth century, it developed
into the term for paying the agent in return for fulfilling
his commission, on the basis of a percentage of the *Gross*
amount.

Commissioners of Inland Revenue
Senior civil servants responsible for managing the assessment
and collection of income tax. They also advise the Treasury
about new taxes and make estimates for the Budget as to
how much tax revenue is likely to be in the coming year.
The actual work of assessing tax is carried out by *Inspectors
of Taxes*, and collection by *Collectors of Taxes*. See also
*General Commissioners, Inland Revenue, Special
Commissioners*.

Committee of London Clearing Banks
A co-ordinating group for the domestic banks, including
Barclays, Lloyds, Midland, National Westminster and
Royal Bank of Scotland. Also part of the network are
subsidiaries of these groups such as Coutts and Williams and
Glyn's. Acts as a pressure group in dealings with the Bank
of England and the Treasury. Talks to the public through
the *Banking Information Service*. The CLCB is based at 10
Lombard Street, London EC3V 9AP.

Commodity
Although it can refer to anything that has a use, the word
is used in business to cover raw materials which are traded in
specialised markets such as bullion, metals, cocoa, sugar,
tea and potatoes. See also *Futures*.

Common Agricultural Policy
An important part of the European Community system –
and a bitter bone of contention. Largely initiated by
France, which has one of Europe's biggest farming lobbies,
the CAP aims to smooth the prices of dairy produce and
wine. They are fixed by the European Commission in
Brussels, which then buys produce if the market prices
fall and charges tariffs on imports from outside the
Community to ensure that they cannot undercut. The effect
has been to encourage overproduction, hence the wine lakes
and butter mountains which occur. The CAP is unpopular
in Britain because it deprives us of the cheap dairy produce

we used to get from Australia and New Zealand. See *Green pound*.

Common Market See *European Community*.

Community Industry
Set up in 1972, this is a scheme designed to help 'socially and personally disadvantaged' people aged 16 to 18 to find work through temporary jobs, mainly in local council workshops. It is run by the National Association of Youth Clubs, but the money comes from the *Manpower Services Commission*.

Community Programme
A *Manpower Services Commission* scheme to give temporary work to jobless people, helping on projects designed to benefit the community, save energy and improve the environment. Companies can put up sponsorship money, and some training is given. The programme is restricted to people between 18 and 24 who have been out of work for more than six months, and over-24s who have been jobless for over a year. It replaced the *Special Temporary Employment Programme*. More details from the MSC, Moorfoot, Sheffield S1 4PQ.

Companies House
Part of the Department of Trade and Industry. All *Limited companies* are required to file their name, address and shareholders, as well as regular sets of accounts. The main registry is at Crown Way, Maindy, Cardiff CF4 3UZ, but there is also a search room at 55 City Road, London EC1Y 1BB. Both are open to the public. There is a separate registry for Scottish companies, in Edinburgh.

Company director
There are three ways of defining a company director. He may be a member of a board of directors elected to manage a company. He may be the sole director of a company. Or,

if the company is managed by the members or owners of
the company, they may all be considered directors.

Company Pensions Information Centre
Based at 7 Old Park Lane, London W1Y 3LJ, this centre
publishes a range of leaflets on aspects of *Occupational
pensions* – including how to understand yours.

Compensation
This covers any attempt to make amends for a misfortune
or wrongdoing, and nowadays almost always takes the
form of money. *Compensation for loss of office* is a legal phrase
referring to any payment made for a dismissal or loss of
working rights which could have been taken to court, even
if it was not. Some of it may be taxable. It is a form of
Damages. See also *Ex-gratia payment*.

Compensation for loss of office
A system which has from time to time been so corrupt that
the payment has been dubbed a golden handshake, or
golden parachute. Payments up to £25,000 are tax-free,
under the Finance Act 1981. Payments over £75,000 can be
taxed in full. Between the two amounts, the tax is graded.
There are also several exemptions, covering payments
made on the death of or injury to the employee, the ending
of the job, payments under approved pension schemes,
and payments by and to non-residents.

Completion See *Exchange of Contracts*.

Composite insurance companies
This describes the all-rounders of the insurance business,
the firms which deal in a variety of different types of insurance
instead of specialising in life, say, or motor. Some of the
biggest insurers on the stock market, such as Commercial
Union, Legal and General and Royal Insurance, are
composites. Their spread of interests should enable them
to even out the risks they take on, but in times of high

inflation it has been difficult for premiums on accident
and repair policies to keep up with payments. They have
had to rely on income from their own investments to stay
ahead of the game.

Composite rate
This is a rate of income tax paid by banks and building
societies on behalf of savers. To save paperwork, the
Inland Revenue calculates the total tax payable on interest
on deposit and saving accounts, which the banks and building
societies hand over as a lump sum. Higher rate tax is paid
on top by individuals.

Composition fee
A facility offered by some private schools as a way of paying
the fees. Parents pay the fees in advance, and they are
then invested by the school in some form of *Annuity*. See
Independent schools information service, School fees insurance.

Compound interest
If you lend £100 at 10% a year *Simple interest*, but do not
collect the interest until the loan ends, the borrower has had
the use of that interest money. It is usual then to pay interest
on the interest, compounding it. After a year, £10 interest
is due. If that is not paid, in the second year there will be
10% interest, or £1, due on that £10 – in addition to the
second year's interest on the original £100, making £121 in
all. But if the loan continues, at the end of year three,
there will be £100 + £10 + £21 + £2.10, totalling £133.10.
Simple interest on £100 at 10% over the three years would
be £30, a difference of £3.10.

Comprehensive insurance See *Motor insurance.*

Conciliation officer
If you apply to an *Industrial tribunal*, your papers
automatically go to your local conciliation officer, who is
part of the government's *Advisory, Conciliation and*

Arbitration Service. He will try to reach a settlement before the case comes before the tribunal.

Confederation of British Industry

This is Britain's main body representing employers. Its members are companies, who use the CBI to lobby government in similar fashion to the TUC on behalf of the unions. The CBI has an elected president and a full-time director-general. Its address is Centre Point, New Oxford Street, London WC1A 1DU.

Consequential dismissal

This is effectively a form of *Redundancy*. It happens if you volunteer for redundancy and someone else takes your job because of a reorganisation. It is no longer the job that has gone – only you. Someone else's job has presumably gone instead.

Consideration

A Stock Exchange nicety stemming from contract law, meaning what you actually pay or receive when you buy or sell *Securities* – net of commission, VAT and other minor considerations.

Constant attendance allowance

Payable only to those people assessed at 100% disability for the purposes of receiving *Disablement benefit*. The victim must be in need of continual care. Someone who is blinded may need this during the early months while he or she adjusts. See *Exceptionally severe disablement*.

Constructive dismissal

This is one of the few cases where an employee can quit a job voluntarily and still claim to have been dismissed. It arises if an employer wants to get rid of one of his people without paying *Compensation* or the *Statutory redundancy payment*. He may move the luckless employee sideways, or just make life unpleasant. In extreme cases, an *Industrial*

tribunal will agree that it amounts to *Unfair dismissal*, but
the employee must have been working for the same employer
for a year, or two years in firms of fewer than 20 people.

Consumer Advice Centre
There is a chain of these centres round the country, run by
either local authorities or the Consumers' Association.
They have a trained staff to give you advice and information.
Some are called Consumer Aid Centres. See also *Citizens'
Advice Bureau.*

Consumer Credit Act
This act, which took effect during 1981, governs the whole
business of lending to the public. It lays down how interest
charges should be presented, and every lender has to be
approved by the Director-General of the *Office of Fair
Trading*, who can withdraw that approval if he finds a lender
has broken the law. You are allowed a 'cooling-off' period,
when you can decide not to go ahead with a finance contract
you have signed. Credit go-betweens, such as mortgage
brokers, estate agents and car salesmen, are also within the
scope of the Act. See *Annual percentage rate*, *True rate*, *Flat
rate*.

Consumer law
Apart from a Victorian rap on the knuckles from the *Sale
of Goods Act*, British shopkeepers were until the 1960s
largely untouched by the law and consumers were left to
fend for themselves under the Latin tag of *Caveat emptor*.
But that began to change with the *Consumer Protection Act*
1961, followed by the Misrepresentation Act 1967, Trade
Descriptions Act 1968, and Unsolicited Goods and Services
Act 1971. The full flowering of consumerism arrived with
the formation of the *Office of Fair Trading* in 1973, ushering
in the Supply of Goods (Implied Terms) Act that same year,
the Consumer Credit Act in 1974, the Unfair Contract Terms
Act 1977 and the Supply of Goods and Services Act 1982.
See also *Consumer Advice Centre*, *Mutual Aid Centre*, *National*

Federation of Consumer Groups, Trading Standards Department.

Consumer Protection Act
This is an Act enabling the government to set safety standards for goods through regulations covering the way they are packed, labelled or made. Like many *Consumer laws*, it does not cover sales by private citizens, so beware the classified ads. Scrap, some damaged goods and goods for export are also outside this law. The Act is particularly concerned with goods for children, such as toys, nightdresses, carry-cots, fireguards and anorak hoods. Electrical goods, oil heaters and kitchen equipment are also regulated. Go to your *Trading Standards Department* if you think the law has been broken.

Contango
If you want to delay paying for shares, your broker can for a small fee arrange a contango, which allows you to carry the bargain over to the next Stock Exchange account. That will give you at least another fortnight before you have to complete the deal – and by then you might have made enough profit to sell anyway. But be careful: you can contango a share only if it is quite heavily traded. See also *Backwardation*.

Continuous balance accounts
As quill pens wore out and Bob Cratchit's successors fell off their high stools, mechanised *ledger* systems took over – now refined by computers. They can strike a balance after each *Transaction*, which would have been a time-wasting exercise for a human bookkeeper. Each line contains the date, details, debit or credit, balance and a reference number, giving a continuous picture at a glance. See *Bookkeeping*.

Contract month
In *Futures* markets, the contract month is the one when a

Futures contract matures, triggering delivery of the item or security in question. It is also known as the delivery month. See also *Delivery notice*, *Delivery point*.

Contracting out
Employers are supposed to contribute to their employees' *Additional component* to the *State pension*. But they can contract out if they have an *Occupational pension* scheme giving something at least as good. This is known as the guaranteed minimum pension and must be frozen for early leavers until they reach State pension wage.

Contractual overtime
This is *Overtime* which is guaranteed by an employer as a regular feature of a worker's employment. It need not be written into the contract of employment. The key difference between contractual and non-contractual overtime is that payment for it is made whether or not the work is done. Another sign is if an employee is disciplined for not working overtime. If that happens, it is contractual.

Control account
As a double check, to save time and cut down the risk of error, bookkeepers have a series of control accounts alongside their normal ones. Each one is really a cross-section through the books. One method is to take groups of accounts starting with the same letter of the alphabet and total the account items on a continuous running balance. At the end of the day the control accounts should agree with the main accounts.

Controlled tenancy See *Regulated tenancy*.

Convertibles
To Americans, these are soft-top cars. But in financial circles they are a type of loan stock which carries the right to convert all or part into shares on prearranged terms. They are issued by companies which do not want to flood the

market with their shares – or want to make a takeover
without giving too much voting power to investors in the
firm being acquired. The rate of interest offered is lower
than it would be on a conventional loan stock. If the
company declines, the conversion rights can become
worthless.

Conveyancing
This is the branch of the law which deals with the transfer
of title deeds to property – in most people's experience,
buying and selling a house. All solicitors are equipped to
handle conveyancing, and that is where you are generally
recommended to go. But in recent years, critics of solicitors'
fees have argued that you can do the conveyancing
yourself. The Consumers' Association publishes guides for
the layman, and there are conveyancing firms who claim
to do the work cheaper than a solicitor. But beware: some
solicitors insist on dealing only with other solicitors, a
point of principle which could cost you your dream house.
See *Law Society*, *National Association of Conveyancers*.

Cooling-off period
Since 1980, anyone who takes out a *Life insurance* policy is
allowed 10 days to change his or her mind. The 10 days
can start from the day the proposal form is signed, but some
firms begin it only when the would-be policyholder
receives the full quotation. Everything paid before the end
of the cooling-off period is repayable.

Copeck See *Kopek*.

Copyright
Literally, the right to copy an original work. Copyright
always begins in the hands of the artist or author, but may be
sold for a *Royalty*, or transferred to a publisher as a condition
of employment. Copyright may also be divided among
different owners for different territories.

Cordoba
The currency of Nicaragua in Central America. Worth about
2p.

Corporate finance
This covers the whole range of types of *Finance* for
companies. It is a speciality of the City's *Merchant banks*,
who earn their fees by putting together the right corporate
finance package for the company in question at any given
time. The range includes *Loans*, *Bills of exchange*, Stock
Exchange *Flotations* of *Shares* or *Debentures*, as well as
Leasing and *Mergers*.

Corporation tax
A tax on UK companies' profits. It was unveiled in the 1965
Budget by James Callaghan, and made an important
distinction between companies and individuals as taxpayers.
Previously they had both paid income tax, but firms also
paid a separate profits tax. From 1965 companies paid their
own corporation tax, and then shareholders paid income
tax on dividends. This led to criticism that shareholders
were being taxed twice – they own the companies, after
all – so the system was modified in 1973 with the invention
of *Imputation tax*.

Cost of manufactured goods account
This is a preliminary account in the process of working out
a *Balance sheet* for a manufacturing firm. It includes *Prime
costs*, *Overheads* and *Work in progress*. See *Manufacturing
account*.

Cost of sales
This is the *Cost of stock sold*, plus whatever it cost to handle
that stock – paying for warehousing and delivery.

Cost of stock sold
When a bookkeeper is calculating a firm's *Trading account*,
the cost of stock sold is the cost of stock held at the start

of the period under review, plus any more bought since
then, minus the cost of whatever is left unsold. See *Cost of
sales*.

Council for Small Industries in Rural Areas
CoSIRA, as it is known, is a government body designed to
revive business in rural areas and towns with a population of
under 10,000. It gives advice, loans and training courses for
employees. It is geared to dealing with 'first-time'
businessmen and their special problems, as well as existing
firms with up to 20 skilled workers. The main office is at
141 Castle Street, Salisbury, Wiltshire SP1 3TP, and they
can put you in touch with a branch near you. See also *New
Enterprise Programme, Small Business Course, Small Firms
Service, Business Expansion Scheme*.

Council for the Securities Industry
The CSI was set up by the Bank of England in 1978 and
wound up in 1986. It is a voluntary body which aims to
maintain standards in the securities industry, investigate
misconduct, resolve differences within the industry,
consider changes in the law and liaise with the European
Community's executive in Brussels. Many of its functions
have been taken over by the Securities and Investments
Board.

Council houses See *Right to buy*.

Council loans fund
This is the central fund which a council uses to finance the
capital spending of its departments, saving those departments
the trouble of each borrowing the money for themselves.
Some money comes from the *Public Works Loans Board*
of the government, but much comes from financial
institutions and from adverts in the newspapers asking the
public to lend.

Counselling
If you are thrown out of work, or about to be, counselling

is the word for a range of help and advice on getting a new job and reshuffling your finances. A good company or trades union should organise this for you. Otherwise it is worth contacting the *British Association for Counselling*.

Coupon
This is the nominal rate of interest attached to a fixed-interest stock, and is worked out on the basis of the stock's nominal value, traditionally £100. What is important to you is the yield on the price you pay, which may be quite different. If you buy a stock for £50, the yield would be double the coupon. If you were to pay £200, the yield would be half the coupon.

Covenant
Coming from the Old French word *convenir*, meaning to agree, a covenant has become a tax device. If you agree to pay a fixed amount to a suitable cause each year, for a number of years, the Inland Revenue will give that cause the *Basic rate* income tax it has collected from you. The most widespread 'suitable cause' is a charity, when the covenant must last for at least four years. In that case, the taxman will actually hand back any *Higher rate* income tax to the donor. It can also be used for grandparents to pay the *School fees* of grandchildren, or for anyone to add to the income of full-time students over 18. In both these cases the covenant must be capable of running for at least six years.

Cover
In insurance, cover is the amount an insurer will pay if an insured event happens. It is agreed when the policy is written, as either a maximum or a minimum figure depending on the type of insurance. Investment-linked life policies often pay more than the sum assured, but insurers like to put a ceiling on accident cover.

Credit cards
When they were introduced into Britain by Barclays Bank

---

in 1966, credit cards were the first new method of storing and using money since the invention of the cheque hundreds of years before. The two biggest in this country are Barclays' Barclaycard, and Access, which is run by the other major banks. They work in virtually the same way. You fill in an application form giving details of your income and debts – you do not have to have a bank account. The cards can be used to buy goods or services wherever their signs are displayed, and the network now covers thousands of shops, garages and restaurants. You can also use them to borrow cash from banks. Each month you are sent a statement of how much you owe, and you must repay at least £5 or 5% of the oustanding debt, whichever is the greater. Interest is charged on anything left unpaid. It can be quite steep, but you effectively get a free loan between the time you buy something and the first date you have to pay for it. That can be up to seven weeks. See also *Debit cards*.

Credit union

This is a type of money club. People who already have some link – through work, hobbies or simply being neighbours – can set up a credit union. There must be between 21 and 5,000 members, each of whom must hold at least one £1 share. They can borrow up to £2,000 more than their shareholding. The snag is that the law bans credit unions from charging more than about 12% a year, or paying more than 8% a year in dividends. In times of high interest rates investors find it hard to resist putting their money elsewhere, especially as there is no guarantee that your local credit union will be particularly well managed. But they are popular abroad, and their very existence will help to keep the banks and building societies on their toes.

Credit Union League of Great Britain

The main organisation promoting the credit union idea in this country. It can give help in explaining the advantages of credit unions, and how to set them up. Its address is PO Box 135, Skelmersdale, Lancashire WN8 8AP.

Creditor

Someone who has given credit, and is therefore owed
something not unakin to money. Creditors are very
reasonably given legal powers to recover their due. It can be
hard to chase a personal debtor, but with companies
creditors have the ultimate sanction: they can apply to put
the firm into liquidation to get at their cash. To prevent a
scrum, the law puts creditors into an orderly queue, starting
with the Inland Revenue and the liquidator himself, closely
followed by those who lent against the security of an asset
such as a property. Shareholders stand at the back of the
line, just behind unsecured or trade creditors.

Cross

This describes the action of a broker in a *Futures* market
who buys and sells the same amount of the same *Futures
contract* at the same price – at the same time. It can make
other brokers cross, too, and they have the right to intervene.
See *Jobber trade*.

Crossed cheque

This is a cheque with two lines drawn across it, north to
south. Between them are usually the words '& Co.', which
was originally a shorthand for the company on whom the
cheque was drawn. Nowadays, it simply means that the
cheque must be paid into another bank account. It cannot
be directly exchanged for cash unless the writer of the
cheque opens it by writing his or her name across it.
In this way, a crossed cheque is less likely to be used
fraudulently.

Cross-tot

When an accounts book is divided into several columns, at
the bottom of each page the columns are totalled and
carried forward to the next page. But, as an extra check,
each line is added crosswise to see if the total agrees in
that direction. This is the cross-tot.

Cruzado
The Brazilian unit of currency. In 1985 there were about 20 to the pound sterling. See *Currency* below.

CSI See *Council for the Securities Industry*.

Cum
When a company announces a dividend, a rights issue or a capitalisation share, a deadline is set for anyone who wants to buy the shares and collect their entitlement to the new feature. Up until that day, the shares are said to be 'cum' – the Latin word for 'with' – the entitlement. Then they go '*Ex*'.

Currency
A currency is another word for money. It covers anything which is used as a medium of exchange, but it normally refers to a nation's monetary unit – pound, dollar, franc, yen and so on. The principal currency of each country is listed below. Individual currencies are entered alphabetically in the rest of the book.

Afghanistan – afghani
Albania – lek
Algeria – dinar
Angola – kwanza
Antigua – dollar
Argentina – austral
Australia – dollar
Austria – schilling
Azores – escudo
Bahamas – dollar
Bahrain – dinar
Balearic Isles – peseta
Bangladesh – taka
Barbados – dollar
Belgium – franc
Belize – dollar
Benin – franc
Bermuda – dollar
Bhutan – ngultrum
Bolivia – peso
Botswana – pula
Brazil – cruzado
British Virgin Isles – dollar
Brunei – dollar
Bulgaria – lev
Burma – kyat
Burundi – franc
Cameroon Republic – franc
Canada – dollar
Canary Islands – peseta
Cape Verde Islands – escudo
Cayman Islands – dollar

Central African Republic –
  franc
Chad – franc
Chile – peso
China – yuan
Colombia – peso
Comoro Islands – franc
Congo – franc
Costa Rica – colon
Cuba – peso
Cyprus – pound
Czechoslovakia – koruna
Denmark – krone
Djibouti – franc
Dominica – dollar
Dominican Republic – peso
Ecuador – sucre
Egypt – pound
Equatorial Guinea – franc
Ethiopia – birr
Falkland Islands – pound
Faroe Islands – krone
Fiji Islands – dollar
Finland – markka
France – franc
French Guiana – franc
French Pacific Islands –
  franc
Gabon – franc
Gambia – dalasi
Germany – mark
Ghana – cedi
Gibraltar – pound
Greece – drachma
Greenland – krone
Grenada – dollar
Guadaloupe – franc
Guam – dollar

Guatemala – quetzal
Guinea Republic – franc
Guinea Bissau – peso
Guyana – dollar
Haiti – gourde
Honduras Republic –
  lempira
Hong Kong – dollar
Hungary – forint
Iceland – krona
India – rupee
Indonesia – rupiah
Iran – rial
Iraq – dinar
Irish Republic – punt
Israel – shekel
Italy – lira
Ivory Coast – franc
Jamaica – dollar
Japan – yen
Jordan – dinar
Kampuchea – riel
Kenya – shilling
Kiribati – dollar
Korea – won
Kuwait – dinar
Laos – kip
Lebanon – pound
Lesotho – maluti
Liberia – dollar
Libya – dinar
Liechtenstein – franc
Luxembourg – franc
Macau – pataca
Madeira – escudo
Malagasy Republic – franc
Malawi – kwacha
Malaysia – ringgit

Maldive Islands – rufiyaa
Mali Republic – franc
Malta – pound
Martinique – franc
Mauritania – ouguiya
Mauritius – rupee
Mexico – peso
Miquelon – franc
Monaco – franc
Mongolia – turgrik
Montserrat – dollar
Morocco – dirham
Mozambique – metical
Nauru – dollar
Nepal – rupee
Netherlands – guilder
Netherlands Antilles – guilder
New Zealand – dollar
Nicaragua – cordoba
Niger Republic – franc
Nigeria – naira
Norway – krone
Oman – rial
Pakistan – rupee
Panama – balboa
Papua New Guinea – kina
Paraguay – guarani
Peru – inti
Philippines – peso
Pitcairn Islands – pound and dollar
Poland – zloty
Portugal – escudo
Puerto Rico – dollar
Qatar – ryal
Réunion – franc
Romania – leu

Rwanda – franc
St Christopher – dollar
St Helena – pound
St Lucia – dollar
St Pierre – franc
St Vincent – dollar
Salvador – colón
Samoa – dollar
San Marino – lira
Sao Tomé – dobra
Saudi Arabia – ryal
Senegal – franc
Seychelles – rupee
Sierra Leone – leone
Singapore – dollar
Solomon Islands – dollar
Somali Republic – shilling
South Africa – rand
Spain – peseta
Sri Lanka – rupee
Sudan Republic – pound
Surinam – guilder
Swaziland – lilangeni
Sweden – krona
Switzerland – franc
Syria – pound
Taiwan – dollar
Tanzania – shilling
Thailand – baht
Togo Republic – franc
Tonga Islands – palanga
Trinidad – dollar
Tunisia – dinar
Turkey – lira
Turks and Caicos Islands – dollar
Tuvalu – dollar
Uganda – shilling

United States – dollar
Uruguay – peso
United Arab Emirates –
    dirham
USSR – rouble
Upper Volta – franc
Vanuatu – vatu
Vatican – lira
Venezuela – bolivar

Vietnam – dong
Virgin Islands – dollar
Western Samoa – tala
Yemen (North) – ryal
Yemen (South) – dinar
Yugoslavia – dinar
Zaire Republic – Zaire
Zambia – kwacha
Zimbabwe – dollar

Current account
One of those financial phrases with a double meaning, one
for banking and the other for the *Balance of payments*. The
current account of the balance of payments displays a
country's exports of goods and services against its imports.
Goods are known here as visibles and services as invisibles,
which include tourism, insurance, shipping, rock stars'
earnings abroad and dividend payments across frontiers.

A bank current account is the basic cheque-drawing
account, where you can expect to draw out virtually any
sum on demand. There is also no limit to what you can put
in, but once you have enough to cover everyday needs you
should consider opening a *Deposit account*. The US version
of a current account is called a demand deposit.

Current cost accounting
When inflation roared out of control in the 1970s,
accountants realised that company profit statements were
becoming fairy tales. The profits were not real because they
were being eaten by rising prices, which put up the cost
of replacing everything from paperclips to old machines. So
they worked out some wonderfully complicated ways of
letting the current costs show through. Unfortunately, they
could not agree amongst themselves about the best way to
go about it, and company directors did not like being told
that their lovely profits were a mirage. But the *Institute of
Chartered Accountants* insisted on firms publishing two sets
of accounts, using both the old and the new methods.

Current cost operating profit
The trading surplus of a business after allowing for the impact of price changes on the money needed to keep the business going at its existing size. It does not matter whether that money comes from *Share* capital or borrowing. This profit is struck before interest and tax.

Current cost profit attributable to shareholders
The profit of a business, after allowing for the effect of price changes on *Shareholders' funds*. It is struck after interest, tax and any one-off items.

Current ratio
This is one of the ratios used to gauge the financial health of a company. The current ratio shows whether a firm's easily-cashed assets match its current liabilities. The assets used are the current assets shown in the balance sheet, minus stocks, on the grounds that the company cannot trade at all without stocks. See *Working capital ratio*, *Acid test*.

Custom
In the financial sense, a custom is a form of *Duty*, one which is levied on goods as they pass a certain point. In the old days, lords would charge customs on goods going to market. Now, however, it is confined to goods entering or leaving the country.

Customs and Excise Department
Based at King's Beam House, Mark Lane, London EC3R 7HE, this is the department which collects *Duty* on alcohol, petrol, tobacco and listed imports. It is also responsible for *Value-Added Tax*.

Dalasi
The currency unit of Gambia, the West African country. The dalasi is worth about 25p.

Damages
A damage is a loss or injury. In the legal sense, damages are

the cash value of the loss. This can be agreed by the injured and the injurer, or it may have to go to court for a verdict. Damages are akin to *Compensation*, except that they tend not to be taxable.

Day book
Every business should have a day book to note the *Original documents* generated by each *Transaction*. These documents are recorded in the order in which they are received, before being copied into the various account books. A large business will have different day books for sales, purchases, returns and fixed assets. See *Bookkeeping*.

Day order
An investment order which has to be completed that day. If not, it is automatically cancelled. See *Fill or kill, Good till cancelled, Limit order, Market order*.

Day trading
If you open and close a *Position* on a financial market in the same day, that is day trading. You may buy a stock and then sell it, or vice versa, so long as you are counting your winnings or losses at the end of the day.

Death Duty See *Inheritance Tax*.

Death grant
A flat cash payment designed to ensure that everyone gets a decent burial. The trouble is that the grant has been left at £30 for so long that it bears no relation to the cost of a modern funeral. The government is thinking about increasing it, however. If you find yourself in the sad position of having to organise a funeral, the undertaker will normally make sure you have the right forms to claim the grant. See also *Industrial death, Widow's allowance, Widow's pension, Widowed mother's allowance*.

Debenture
A grand word for a loan. Debentures are loans raised by

companies with a property as security. That is why they are sometimes known as mortgage debentures. Because of their status, debentures are the first of all loans to be repaid when a company is liquidated.

Debit cards
These are the next step on from credit cards. Using a microchip, they could be issued by banks with a preset spending power in them. Every time you used the card, what you spent would be electronically 'knocked off', until there was nothing left. Some people may be more at ease with debit cards than credit cards, as you obviously cannot run up a huge bill which you can't pay.

Debt
If you owe it, it's a debt.

Debt/equity ratio
A device for analysing balance sheets. If you look at the liabilities or 'capital employed' side of the accounts, you will see that it is made up broadly of shareholders' funds – equity – and loan capital. It is not a bad idea for most well-managed companies to borrow some money. But if the debts grow too big, the burden of interest payments will crowd out dividends and turn into more of a hindrance than a help. Ideally, equity and debt should be about equal, but it can vary widely from industry to industry. It is worth checking the position in a cross-section of similar firms. Then see how your company matches up.

Debtor
Someone who owes, usually money.

Decimal currency
The system whereby the main currency unit is divided into 100 subsidiary units for more precise pricing. 'Decimal' is strictly a misnomer as it refers to tenths, but the term was adopted to contrast with the duodecimal system which was

in use in Britain and much of the Commonwealth until the early 1970s. Britain converted to decimal currency on 15 February 1971.

Deep discount bonds See *Zero coupon bonds*.

Defalcation
Money stolen from a business by a trusted employee. See *Embezzlement, Fidelity bond*.

Deferred
Anything that is put off: in money terms, a delayed liability, whether it be tax or shares or creditors. Chancellors are loath to admit mistakes, so they sometimes defer a tax instead of abolishing it, and that is how it has to appear in balance sheets. Deferred shares usually do not earn a dividend for several years, and they may not carry votes during that time, either. Deferred creditors simply wait for their money.

Deferred futures
The most distant months of a *Futures contract*, as opposed to *Nearby futures*.

Deferred pension
This is what you can get if you leave a job after working in it for at least five years. You can take the money out. See also *Normal retirement age* and *Occupational pension* scheme.

Deflation
This is the opposite of *Inflation*. It refers to a general fall in wages and prices, so that each pound becomes worth more. In its way, it can be just as misleading and unsettling as inflation and is believed to be more likely to cause unemployment because people will have a reason to delay buying things: tomorrow they may be cheaper.

Deliverable name
When a commodity or security has to be delivered at the

end of a *Futures contract*, it has to have a deliverable name,
in that it must be one of a range of *Financial instruments*
which meet that particular order. See *Delivery*.

Delivery
The physical handover of a *Security*, *Commodity* or other
Financial instrument to settle a contract. See *Delivery notice*,
Delivery point.

Delivery month See *Contract month*.

Delivery notice
When a seller intends to deliver a *Commodity* or *Financial
instrument*, he sends the buyer a notice that *Delivery* will
take place on a given date. This can act as a warning to a
'buyer' who was really only speculating on the price and
does not intend to be landed with the goods.

Delivery point
Futures markets name certain places where *Commodities* or
Financial instruments may be delivered. When they have
reached that point, the contract is legally fulfilled.

Demand
In economic terms, the only demand that matters is the one
backed by the money to pay for it. Economic theory assumes
that demand for anything falls as the price rises, and rises
as the price falls. See *Economics*, *Elasticity*, *Price*, *Supply*,
Macro-economics, *Micro-economics*.

Demand deposit See *Current account*.

Demerger
This is where part of a *Group* of companies is split off from
the rest. While this sounds easy, in practice it was almost
impossible until the tax laws were changed in the 1980
Finance Act. Now, under certain conditions, a demerger can
take place free of most taxes and *Stamp duty*. But, to

complicate matters, measures have been built in to stop firms
from demerging simply to avoid tax. Essentially, the Inland
Revenue has to be convinced that a demerger is genuine.

Demonstrative legacy

A *Legacy* in which the *Testator* says where the money is to
come from to pay the gift. If you, making the *Will*, have some
building society savings and some shares in your family
business, you may want the shares to go to your eldest
son. To ensure that the shares are untouched, you stipulate
that a legacy of £100 to cousin Mabel must come out of
the building society money.

Denarius

The smallest unit of the pre-1971 British currency system
of pound, shilling, penny. Like the other terms, it had
Latin origins. Ironically, in view of the eventual switch to
Decimal currency, the denarius was in Roman times worth
ten asses. But in Britain it became equal to a pennyworth,
or a 240th, of a pound of silver. It is also related to the
middle eastern *Dinar*.

Departmental accounts

Companies often like to have separate accounts for each
department, so that they can see more clearly what is
happening – and if one department is doing much worse
than the others. It can also help to spot fraud or theft, and
show which products are selling best.

Dependent relative allowance

This is a tax allowance for people who maintain either a
relative who cannot take care of himself or herself, or a
widowed mother or mother-in-law. If the dependent relative
has an income, the allowance is cut £ for £ by the extent
to which it exceeds the basic retirement pension. The
allowance is also restricted to the amount the claimant
spends, up to a declared limit. Ask your local Inland
Revenue office for details. The address is in the phone
book.

Deposit account
An account with a bank from which money can be drawn
only after a period of notice, usually seven days. In return
for this inconvenience, money in the account carries interest.
Some banks offer extra interest if more than £10,000 is
deposited. In the US, this facility is known as a time deposit.

Deposit box
The nearest thing to *Numbered bank accounts* in this country.
For a fee you can have your own deposit box in a bank, where
you can keep just about anything so long as it is not animal,
vegetable or likely to cause damage . . . and the banks do
not want to know. Best, though, to take out *All-risks
insurance* in case the bank is robbed.

Deposit protection scheme
Under the *Banking Act 1979*, both *Recognised banks* and
Licensed deposit-takers must contribute to this scheme. If one
of them goes bust, the customers should get back £7,500 of
the first £10,000 of any sterling deposits.

Depreciation
When you use a machine, wear and tear eventually cuts its
value to scrap. Companies show this in balance sheets
under depreciation. The wear and tear is turned into a cash
sum, normally by deciding how long each machine's life
is and lopping a regular amount each year. The period can
vary from three years for cars to 50 years or more for
buildings. In theory, this gives the company a fund with
which to buy new machinery. But inflation has meant that
the cost of replacement has rocketed, distorting the picture
for many firms. And it is very much a matter of opinion
how long it will be before a piece of equipment is obsolete.
See *Diminishing balance method*, *Straight line method*.

Depression
A depression is a sinking of the economy and a low point in
activity, when machines, men and money all stand

relatively idle and no one can see a way out. Up to the time of writing, though, depressions have eventually melted as the *Trade cycle* has slowly spun round to a *Boom*. The pit of an unusually bad depression is called a *Slump*. See also *Recession*.

Devaluation
Once a taboo word in financial circles, it became less emotive in the 1970s when major currencies were allowed to float on foreign exchange markets. Before that, exchange rates were fixed. If a currency became overvalued, there had to be a formal devaluation by the government – usually after a torrent of rumours. That is what happened to the pound in 1967.

Devise
A legal term for giving a *Legacy* of freehold property to a beneficiary of a *Will*. It also refers to the clause in the will setting out the terms of the legacy.

Difference account
When an investor *Closes a position*, his or her broker sends an account for the difference between the buying and selling price, with a cheque – or a demand.

Diminishing balance method
A *Depreciation* technique. The value of an asset is depreciated by a fixed percentage every year. But the asset is never completely written off unless a floor value is brought in. Then when the value goes below the floor it can be regarded as worthless. Another snag is that it works very unevenly if the firm wants to depreciate something over a short period, like three years. See *Revaluation period, Straight line method*.

Dinar
Of Persian origin, the dinar has been adopted by several middle eastern countries, as well as Algeria, Libya, Tunisia and Yugoslavia. The dinars of Bahrain, Iraq, Jordan,

Kuwait, Libya and South Yemen are worth between £1.50 and £2. The Algerian version costs about 12p, and the Yugoslavian a fifth of a penny. The Tunisian dinar is about par with the pound. See *Denarius*.

Direct debit
This is a way of paying regular bills. You give the recipient – gas or electricity board, local council, insurance firm – the right to take an agreed sum out of your bank account on certain dates. This is tending to take over from *Standing orders*, because it means less paper work. In its original and extreme form, the recipient had the right to take any sum out of your account, an innovation which produced innumerable foul-ups in the early days. Most firms asking for a direct debit facility say they will always check with you before they alter the amount they are extracting. Make sure they do.

Direct expenses
In factory businesses, costs are divided between direct and indirect, or *Overheads*. The direct costs, also known as prime or variables, include raw materials and wages. They vary directly with the amount of work being done. In theory, *Depreciation* on machines falls into this group, but some accountants treat it as an overhead. See *Manufacturing accounts*.

Direct tax
A tax, such as *Income tax* or *Inheritance Tax*, which is paid directly to the government by those who are liable to pay it, under a formula laid out in the Finance Acts. See also *Indirect tax*.

Direct training service
This is a service provided by the *Manpower Services Commission*. It offers training programmes to companies, in return for which the firms must pay part of the cost. Some courses are held at the workplace by mobile instructors,

while others take place at instructor training colleges or Skillcentres. Details can be had from the MSC at Moorfoot, Sheffield S1 4PQ.

Director See *Company director, Institute of Directors.*

Directors' report
By law, this has to appear with the annual accounts of every limited company. It contains a list of statutory information, including the activities of the firm, its directors' shareholdings, the number and pay of employees, any political or charitable contributions and any major changes in the company since the last report.

Dirham
Like *Drachma*, 'dirham' stems from the Greek verb 'to grasp', and is related to the Scots dram. It is the currency of the two states at the eastern and western ends of the Arab world – the United Arab Emirates and Morocco. The Moroccan dirham is worth around 10p, and the UAE version 20p.

Disability benefit
There are several benefits paid by the government to help meet the extra costs of various types of handicap. The local social security office or *Citizens' Advice Bureau* should be able to advise whether you or someone you know would qualify. In many areas there are also legal advice centres which specialise in helping people to collect their entitlement. See *Attendance allowance, Blind person's allowance, Dependent relative allowance, Disablement benefit, Injury benefit, Invalid care allowance, Invalidity pension* and *Mobility allowance.*

Disabled
There is a range of employment schemes and tax concessions to help disabled people. See *Attendance allowance, Blind allowance, Disablement benefit, Mobility allowance, Fit for*

Work Campaign, Employment Rehabilitation Centre, Sheltered employment, Remploy.

Disablement benefit
This is paid if you lose a physical or mental faculty through an industrial accident or *Disease*. You do not have to have claimed *Sickness benefit* or *Injury benefit*, and you may go back to work. The payment depends on the degree of disablement, expressed as a percentage and assessed by a medical board. You have the right of appeal. As a guide, the loss of both hands is 100% disablement, one hand 60%. Blindness also rates 100%. Over 20% – loss of a couple of fingers – a weekly pension is paid, below 20% you get a once-for-all lump sum. Several extra payments can be made: see *Constant attendance allowance, Exceptionally severe disablement, Hospital treatment allowance, Special hardship allowance, Unemployability allowance.*

Discount
This applies to a stock or share whose value has fallen. A share which has fallen faster than most is said to be at a discount against the market. But there is also a *Discount market* in the City, operated by firms called discount houses. They deal in bills, which are promises to pay a few months hence. If the creditor does not want to wait that long, he sells the bill. But there is a price for his impatience: the bill is bought at a discount, roughly equal to the current rate of interest for the period. The government is a big seller of *Treasury bills* to the discount market.

Discount brokerage See *Execution only*.

Discount card
A form of consumer club. You buy membership for a yearly fee, in return for which you are entitled to discounts at an agreed list of shops. The shops join the scheme in the hope that it will bring them extra business. Before joining, you should try to work out if you are going to save more in those shops than the cost of the annual fee.

Discount market
Due to become defunct as a separate market under the new rules for the Gilts market in 1986, it was used by the Bank of England for 160 years as a means of regulating interest rates.

Discretionary accounts
These are accounts operated by *Stockbrokers* for their clients. Where the client does not want to be consulted about every transaction carried out on his behalf, he can give the broker discretion to deal first and report back later. This can also happen when the client is not always available, so that the broker would otherwise be unable to take advantage of fast-moving events. Or it may be that the *Portfolio* is so small that it would be too expensive to check on every deal. But see *Churning*.

Disease
If caught at work, a disease can rate for either *Injury benefit* or *Disablement benefit*. But it must be a listed disease contracted in an occupation listed under the industrial injuries scheme. Full details of the scheme can be had from your local social security office or *Citizens Advice Bureau*. The ailments include anthrax, chemical poisoning, radiation sickness, tuberculosis resulting from contact with a patient and dust-related diseases.

Disinvestment
When a firm buys more factories and machinery, it is investing. If it sells those things, or lets them wear out, that is disinvestment.

Dismissal
If you leave a job on your employer's say-so, whatever the reason, in law you have been dismissed. This is so even if the employer has asked for volunteers for *Redundancy*.
However, the law recognises several other types of dismissal, some of which qualify for *Compensation*. See *Consequential dismissal, Constructive dismissal, Unfair dismissal*.

Whichever it is, you are legally entitled to a written
explanation of the reasons from your employer.

Dissaving
If you spend more than you earn, you are dissaving, either
by drawing on your savings or by borrowing.

Distribution
This has three quite separate but connected meanings.
Traditionally distribution refers to the business of taking
goods from the farms and factories to the consumer, through
the complex network of wholesalers and retailers – known
as the distributive trades. Distribution also has a legal
meaning for tax reasons, covering the process of
distributing a company's dividends or assets among its
shareholders. Thirdly, it is a word used by followers of share
Charts to say that people have been selling.

Dividend cover
The net profits of a company, divided by the net cost of the
dividend declared. This is how to find out whether a company
can really afford the dividend it is paying – or, alternatively,
whether the directors are being too miserly. If the cover
is below one, then the dividends come to more than the
profits, and the dividend is described as 'uncovered'. A cover
of more than three times is generally regarded as
conservative. The 'net' element in the calculation means
net of tax in both cases.

Dividend mandate
A form which a shareholder fills in if he wants the dividends
on his shares to be paid into a bank or to someone else.
Stockbrokers can normally supply them.

Dividend request form See *Dividend mandate*.

Divorce
Divorce inevitably changes the tax status of both

ex-partners, and you should get advice from your solicitor, or the social security office. The Inland Revenue will not give direct advice, but they do publish a leaflet, IR30, on *Separation and divorce*. See *Maintenance payments, Personal allowances, Separate taxation*.

Dobra

The currency of Sao Tomé and Principé, two islands off Gabon on the West African coast. It comes from the Spanish word *dobla*, meaning a gold coin, and is worth about 2p.

Dollar

The world's most popular currency name. Like the franc, it splits into two main camps and several satellites. Most are tied to the United States dollar, worth around 80p. This group includes Bahamas, Bermuda, British and US Virgin Islands, Guam, Liberia, Puerto Rico, American Samoa and the Turks and Caicos Islands. The other big group consists of those using the East Caribbean dollar costing about 30p: Antigua, Dominica, Grenada, Montserrat, St Christopher, St Lucia and St Vincent. A smaller group is collected round the Australian dollar, worth around 60p. Among them are Kiribati, Nauru, Tuvalu and Vanuatu. The New Zealand dollar is worth about 35p, while the Solomon Islands dollar is close to the Australian. The Canadian dollar used to be closely connected with the US, but it is now worth about 50p. Other dollar nations are Belize (at 3 to the pound), Brunei (about the same), Cayman Islands (worth £1), Fiji (worth 60p), Guyana (5.9 to the pound), Hong Kong (12), Pitcairn Islands (as NZ), Singapore (2.5), Taiwan (50), Trinidad (5.5), Zimbabwe (2) and Jamaica (9). See *Cent*.

Dollar premium

Defunct after exchange controls were abolished in 1979, the dollar premium was a method of putting a price on the limited pool of dollars available for investing overseas. The premium was always quoted as a percentage, based on a fixed rate for the dollar against the pound – latterly 2.60. If

the premium was 80%, and the current market exchange rate
was $2 = £1, the sum worked like this. You add 100 to the
premium, making 180. Multiply that by the exchange rate:
$180 \times 2 = 360$. Divide that by 2.60: 138.4. Subtract 100,
leaving a 'true' premium of 38.4%. This contorted formula
did not apply to holiday money.

Domestic credit expansion
An attempt to produce an uncluttered definition of Money
supply. Propounded by J. J. Polak of the *International Monetary
Fund*, DCE tries to take out foreign influences on a country's
money supply by adding to it any deficit on *Balance of
payments*, or subtracting any surplus. In this way, domestic
economic policies can be more sharply focused. But there
are so many influences on the balance of payments that DCE
can vary wildly – and misleadingly. See *Monetarism*.

Donation
The act of donating, or giving, and the name for what is
given. It comes from the Latin word *donationem*. Someone
who makes a donation is called a donor and, though this is
very rarely used, the person who receives a gift is a donee.

Dong
The dong is the main currency unit of Vietnam, and is worth
about 4p. It is divided into 10 hao, which are in turn
divided into 10 xu. Tourists can get a bonus on the official
exchange rate.

Double-entry bookkeeping
Every business *Transaction* is recorded in the books twice,
because each involves a credit and a debit to different parts of
the business. If a firm buys a van, the cash account is
credited with the cost and the vehicle account is debited
with the same amount. In this way the accountants can make
sure that the books balance. See *Bookkeeping*.

Double taxation
This occurs when a person belongs to one country but lives

in another. Every country taxes its residents, and most also tax their nationals who work abroad. Several pairs of countries have recognised the injustice of this by signing double taxation treaties which try to cancel out the double effect. In some other cases the United Kingdom lets Britons off certain types of income from abroad. Or a UK taxpayer can declare his foreign income net of the foreign tax. The legal Bible on this question is the Income and Corporation Taxes Act 1970.

Double top See *Head and shoulders.*

Doubloon
Made legendary in the days of pirates on the Spanish main, the doubloon is a now-obsolete word for a golden coin dating from 1622. It comes from the French and Spanish word *doblon*, and is also believed to be connected to 'double', as it was worth two pistoles.

Drachma
The Greek currency; its pedigree can be traced back to the word meaning 'to grasp'. Like the British pound, it was originally a measure of weight, surviving in the Scottish 'dram'. The drachma is in turn related to the Arab dirham. The Greek unit is nowadays worth less than ½p.

Dual capacity
From 1911 until 1986 members of the London Stock Exchange had to choose beween acting as brokers and acting as jobbers. They were not allowed to do both. That rule has been abolished, and they can operate in both capacities, except that jobbers are now known as *market makers.*

Dumping
This is a business tactic, where a company sells goods at an artificially low price, either to break into a new market or to stop others from entering the fray. It is a particularly

sensitive matter when the dumping is done by a foreign company.

Duodecimal currency

The currency system which grew up in Britain and was then exported to the former British Empire. Unlike the decimal system, it was based on 12 pennies to a shilling, and 20 shillings to a pound. This was gradually abandoned by the former Empire countries after they achieved independence. Its complexity finally led to its being scrapped by the UK in 1971. See *Libra*, *Solidus*, *Denarius*, *Decimal currency*.

Duty

A payment to the government on the import, export, sale or manufacture of certain goods. In Britain duty is collected by the *Customs and Excise Department*. See *Custom*, *Excise*.

Early retirement

This is not available under the *State pension*, but is possible with an *Occupational pension scheme*. It can be taken at any time if the employee is permanently disabled, otherwise he has to be over 50. The pension is still geared to the number of years of contributions or service.

Earnings

To a worker, his earnings are what he takes home in pay. To a company, it is the figure three lines up from the bottom of the annual profit-and-loss account showing, after tax, interest and all other charges, how much profit the company earned. Below that comes a deduction to pay the shareholders' dividend, and what is left is transferred to reserves. If the numbers are moving the other way, your firm is losing money, not earning.

Earnings related pension

Until 1961 everyone received the same *State pension*, no matter what they had been paid in wages. While this gave pensioners a guaranteed minimum, it meant a big drop in living standards for some. But under the National Insurance Act 1959 employers and employees chipped in a percentage of the employee's pay, within set limits. But this graduated pension plan could not cope with high *Inflation*, so it was frozen in 1975, and replaced three years later by an *Additional component*. See *Pension, State pension, Basic component*.

ECGD See *Export Credits Guarantee Department*.

ECI See *Equity Capital for Industry*.

Econometrics
The statistician's corner in economics. Econometrics attempts to test economic theories by using scientific methods and mathematical models.

Economics
The study of how resources are used, how end-products are distributed, and how they should be distributed. As this obviously shatters the fond illusion that we can all have as much as we want, it is easy to see why it is regarded as the dismal science. See *Demand, Price, Supply, Macro-economics, Micro-economics, Keynes, Classical economics*.

Elasticity
This measures the rate at which the *Supply* of and *Demand* for something respond to changes in *Price*. If a small price-change produces a huge increase in demand or supply, it is said to be elastic. If price makes little difference, the demand for supply is said to be inelastic. Some people will pay anything for a pint of beer, but newspaper circulations can slide on even a penny price rise.

Eligible margin
In *Futures* markets, investors must put down a deposit as a proportion of the value of their *Futures contract*, and may have

to top this up if they chalk up losses. This margin must be paid in cash or some form of *Collateral* specified by the particular exchange. See *Initial margin, Maintenance margin, Variation margin.*

Embezzlement
Theft of money from a business by an employee in a position of trust, such as a cashier. See *Defalcation, Fidelity bond.*

Emergency coding See *Tax codes.*

Employment Fellowship
This group operates an employment bureau for retired people. The scheme is called Buretire and it is involved with firms in many parts of the country. The fellowship's address is Drayton House, 30 Gordon Street, London WC1H 0BE.

Employment Rehabilitation Centre
There is a network of these centres round the country, run by the *Manpower Services Commission* to train people to return to work after a long illness or being handicapped. Apart from helping to restore physical strength and confidence, the centres give guidance on the best type of work for the individuals to aim at. Further information from the MSC, Moorfoot, Sheffield S1 4PQ.

Employment Service Division
The part of the Manpower Services Commission responsible for finding people jobs, running *Job Centres, Professional and Executive Recruitment, Employment Rehabilitation Centres* and schemes for employment of the disabled. See also *Careers and Occupational Information Centre, Employment Transfer Scheme, Job Search Scheme, SEPACS, Community Enterprise Programme, Fit for Work Campaign.*

Employment Transfer Scheme
This is a scheme to help people to move to new jobs in

different parts of the country, largely by paying part of the cost. It is run by the *Manpower Service Commission's Employment Service Division*.

Encumbrace See *Lien*.

Endowment insurance
A form of investment dressed in the garb of a life insurance policy. For a higher premium than, say, *Term insurance*, the policyholder is guaranteed a relatively high 'sum assured' – the minimum to be expected at the end of the policy, or when the named 'life' dies, whichever is the sooner. There is always a payout, because the bulk of the premium is invested. An endowment policy that runs its full course normally pays far more than the sum assured, because of bonuses. This is also partly because the insurance firm sets a cautious sum assured, in case its investments come unstuck.

Endowment mortgage
This is a house *Mortgage* linked to an *Endowment insurance* policy big enough to pay it off. None of the mortgage principal is paid off during the period, as all the payments go to meet mortgage interest and premiums on the insurance. It is no longer regarded as worthwhile because there is no tax relief on premiums since the 1984 Budget. In recent years a 'low-start' endowment mortgage has been introduced, where the initial endowment cover is only a fraction of the mortgage, relying on bonuses to bring the two into line.

Enterprise
A French import meaning an undertaking, 'enterprise' has always had more of a flavour of risk and adventure than the more mundane '*Business*'. Unhappily, instead of calling the hero of such commercial adventures an enterpriser, we fell hook, line and sinker for the inelegant French 'entrepreneur'.

Enterprise Agency
A series of these agencies has been set up round the country.

They are an attempt by large companies to help small
ones, offering training, advice and contact with potential
lenders or investors. If your nearest is not in the phone
book, write to the London Enterprise Agency, 69 Cannon
Street, London EC4N 5AB for the information. See *Council
for Small Industries in Rural Areas, Small Firms Service*.

Enterprise zones
Set up by Sir Geoffrey Howe in his Budget of March 1980,
enterprise zones are selected areas of several hundred acres
which have suffered economic or physical decline. In
England, local authorities suggest sites to the Secretary of
State for the Environment. The Secretaries of State for
Scotland, Wales and Northern Ireland have their own
systems. Any business moving to an enterprise zone gets a
10 – year holiday from rates, development land tax and
industrial training levies, and 100% tax allowances on
buildings. See also *Business Expansion Scheme, Small Firms
Service, CoSIRA, London Enterprise Agency*.

Entertainment See *Business entertaining*.

Entrepreneur See *Enterprise*.

Equal instalment method
This is a method of calculating *Depreciation*. Its other name
is the *Straight line method*.

Equal Opportunities Commission See *Equal Pay Act*.

Equal Pay Act
This Act gives women the right to the same pay and
conditions as men if they are doing similar work or if a
job evaluation scheme has given a woman's job the same
rating as a man's. It tends to be applicable only with jobs in
the same firm or under the same roof. If you are unhappy,
the doors to knock on are, in order of priority: your
employer, trade union, ACAS, *Equal Opportunities*

Commission, solicitor. The Equal Opportunities Commission, Overseas House, Quay Street, Manchester M3 3HN, also supervises the Sex Discrimination Act on job opportunities.

Equity

A handy shorthand for ordinary shares, and the stock market is often called the equity market. But it has a wider meaning, too. You can own the equity in any asset. That means that if its value changes, you take the profit or the loss. That is obviously true if you own the asset outright, but you may have borrowed to buy it – like the mortgage on a house. In that case, the lender receives interest on the loan, and gets his money back at the end. You have the equity. You could even offer a lender a slice of the equity in return for lower interest charges.

Equity Bank See *Equity Capital for Industry*.

Equity Capital for Industry

When Sir Harold Wilson's committee was looking into financial institutions in the 1970s, there was much criticism that the City was not imaginative enough, and worthwhile business schemes were being starved of money because stuffy bankers allegedly would not bend their rules. The bankers did not accept this, but just to meet the point, before Wilson reported they and a couple of dozen pension funds, insurance firms and local authorities put up £40m to start ECI. It was designed specifically to hold shares in companies rather than lend them money. Its record has been patchy, and there have been cries to wind it up, but it has been a convenient place for the banks to send their less healthy corporate customers.

Ernie

The name is an acronym for Electronic Random Number Indicator, a title dreamed up in 1957 when Harold Macmillan was Chancellor of the Exchequer. It is in fact a

computer at Bootle, in Lancashire, where the National
Giro is based. Every month Ernie selects the winning
numbers in the *Premium Bond* draw.

Escalator share

This is one of the more recent types of building society
saving account. It is a refinement of the *Term share*, with some
elements of the *Subscription share* thrown in. The idea is that
the longer you leave the money in an escalator share
account the higher the rate of interest you receive. There
are many permutations on the theme, and the big societies
have criticised one another's versions in their advertising
campaigns. Though the choice can be bewildering the
competition can only be good for the saver.

Escrow

If something is put in escrow, that means it is being parked
until some condition is fulfilled. This can happen if someone
is due to give some money as part of a contract. If there is
a complication, the money may be put in escrow –
deposited with a third party such as a bank – until things
are sorted out.

Escudo

Portugal's main unit of currency, worth less than ½p. It was
originally a Spanish word meaning 'shield'. From there it was
a short step for a shield-bearer to be called an 'escudero',
transformed by wars into the English 'esquire'.

Estate

Although some people think of an estate as a type of car, it
has two other main meanings. An estate often refers to
property, usually an expanse of rolling acres in the
countryside: however, the Grosvenor Estate in Mayfair shows
that there are still one or two in cities. The other meaning
is the total wealth, property and assets of someone who
has died. See *Will*.

Estate agent
Someone who helps you to buy or sell a property, in return
for a percentage of the eventual price. There is no laid-down
scale, but for an ordinary house it should be about 2% or
3%. Estate agents vary in experience and expertise from
the man in a high-street shop to those agents who advertise
mansions in glossy magazines. At present they do not need
any professional qualifications, although there is pressure
for them to do so. But as long as they do not collect any
commission until the deal is signed, they cannot do much
harm, beyond wasting your time. And most do a good job.
See *Multiple agency, Sole agency, Sole selling rights.*

Estate Agents Act
This 1979 Act came into force in May 1982. It gives home
buyers and sellers the right to know in advance an estate
agent's fees and how they will be charged, to have deposits
paid into a special account which may earn interest, and
to know if an estate agent has a personal interest in a property
he is buying or selling. Offending agents can be banned
by the director-general of the *Office of Fair Trading.* A list
of offenders is kept at Government Buildings, Bromyard
Avenue, London W3 7BB.

Estate duty See *Capital Tax.*

Estate income
Income which is liable to tax under *Schedules A, B and D,*
stemming from owning, occupying or having some other
right over land or buildings.

Eurobonds
A means for governments and big multinational companies
to borrow. They are normally denominated in a currency,
usually the most attractive of the moment, and are floated
on the major European stock exchanges. They are also
traded by banks and money brokers. Because they can be
affected by movements both in exchange rates and interest
rates, they are best left to professional investors.

Eurodollars

Originally, a word for US dollars held by Europeans in the 1960s because the dollar was a *Hard currency* which, unlike the Swiss franc, was easy to deal in because it was so widely used in international trade. Now the so-called Eurodollar market deals in bonds denominated in several leading western currencies, even if they are held by the natives of the countries with those currencies. This market works largely on the phone and has the attraction of being multinational, making it difficult for any one government to impose restrictions on it. This can make Eurodollars a haven for *Hot money*.

European Commission

The executive arm of the *European Community*. It is based in Brussels and consists of civil servants led by politicians appointed by the member countries.

European Community

An economic and political union of western European nations. It began in 1957 with the Treaty of Rome, which cut down customs barriers between the original six members. It now includes a *Common Agricultural Policy*, a *European Monetary System* and free movement of labour. By 1986 there were 12 members: Belgium, Denmark, France, Greece, Ireland, Italy, Luxembourg, Netherlands, Portugal, Spain, United Kingdom and West Germany. The Community headquarters are in Brussels.

European Currency Unit

A way of simplifying the horrendously complicated financial problems of the *European Community*, as the common market is now called. Instead of having each member country's currency floating freely, each country haggles to have its rate fixed, purely for the purposes of working out the ECU. Once that is done, the income and spending of the community is calculated in terms of the ECU. See *Green pound*.

European Investment Bank
A *European Community* body, designed to shift money to
regions in need – either because of long-term problems
like unemployment, or to cope with relief from large-scale
disasters.

European Monetary System
The EMS is a first step by the *European Community* towards
a common currency for all the member countries. It works
by linking the currencies to one another in a complex grid,
allowing each of them a small amount of movement against
one another, but letting the whole lot float reasonably freely
against the rest of the world's currencies. This has not
prevented some big readjustments within EMS, and up to
April 1986 Britain had opted out of joining.

Evasion of tax
Tax evasion is outright law-breaking, whether by sending
false returns to the Inland Revenue or simple fiddling. If you
are caught it can mean fines or imprisonment. It is quite
different from *Avoidance of tax*, which is mainly within
the law.

Ex
Shares can go ex-dividend, ex-rights or ex-capitalisation.
The 'ex-' means that the shares no longer carry entitlement to
the facility in question. On that day there will probably be
a drop in the share price to take account of this, and
investors will be warned by the mark xd, xr or xc against
the price in the newspapers.

Exceptionally severe disablement
Someone who will need the *Constant attendance allowance*
permanently may also qualify for a further payment in
respect of exceptionally severe disability. See *Disablement
benefit*.

Excess
Most accident insurance policies carry an excess, which is

an amount the policyholder has to pay before the insurer becomes liable. It is usually in the region of £15, but young or bad drivers can have to pay as much as the first £50 or £100. The main reason for inserting an excess clause is to prevent trivial claims which would cost more to process than they are worth. It also cuts out the majority of accident costs. The other reason, as in the driving case, is if the insurer thinks someone is going to be a bad risk. He is simply telling the policyholder to be more careful than he might otherwise be.

Exchange of contracts

This is the crucial moment in buying a home. After all the preparatory work has been done by the *Building society, Surveyors* and *Solicitors*, and the price has been agreed, under English law you are committed once you have sent a signed copy of the contract to the seller's solicitors. If you then try to back out, you can be sued for the money, and if the house burns down after the exchange of contracts it is your loss – even if you have not had time to move in. The final stage is completion, when the money actually changes hands – in return for the keys to the front door! See *Conveyancing.*

Exchange rate

The value of one currency in terms of another. This is necessary to work out the prices of goods across frontiers, when they become imports and exports. The system which results then becomes a way of encouraging one economy and holding back another through the rise or fall in the value of the different currencies. Governments can normally soften the impact of such shifts if they conflict with national economic policy.

Excise

The Excise is the shorthand name for the *Customs and Excise Department*, which is responsible for collecting excise. This is a form of *Duty*, but it is confined to duty levied on goods

made in Britain, as opposed to imports. The main excise
items are alcohol and tobacco.

Execution only
A no-frills service by a *Broker/dealer*, in which he offers to
do no more than transact deals for a client, without giving
any advice. The advantage to the client is that the *Commission*
rate is lower. This is broadly equivalent to what is known
in the US as discount brokerage.

Executor
Someone appointed by a *Testator* to carry out the instructions
of a *Will*. To do so, after the death of the testator the
executor must apply for *Probate*. If no executor is named,
an administrator applies for grant of letters of administration
with the will attached. If that is granted, the administrator
can then act as executor.

Exempt
To be exempt from something is to be given legal freedom
from liability for it. It is an important part of the *Value-added
tax* laws. Many goods and services are *Zero-rated*. But others,
such as land, insurance, cremation and education, are
exempt. This means that the traders in question cannot
claim VAT refunds on their sales. Consumers at large and
traders below a certain yearly turnover are also exempt.

Exercise
To take up an option to buy or sell shares.

Ex-gratia payment
This is a payment made voluntarily by an employer when
he has ended an employee's contract early. As it is voluntary,
it comes on top of any *Statutory redundancy payment*. Like
Compensation, some of it may be taxable.

Export Credits Guarantee Department
A government department formed in 1930 to help exporters.

Although it is non-profit-making, ECGD effectively acts
as an insurer, charging exporters a premium in return for
guaranteeing that they will get at least part of their money
back on contracts. This lets an exporter know where he
stands, particularly with a new foreign customer. ECGD also
acts as a warning post, for it refuses to guarantee contracts
in certain parts of the world. Its office is at Aldermanbury
House, Aldermanbury, London EC2P 2EL.

Extel Statistical Services
An essential source of information for the serious investor.
It is a card-index system which has data on every company
with a stock market quote, and can cover foreign firms too.
You can buy just one card at a time. The service is based
at 37 Paul Street, London EC2A 4PB.

Factor of production
Economics identifies three classical factors of production:
land, labour and capital. The last can include equipment
and buildings. There is also a fourth, less tangible, factor in
the creative leadership of management in choosing how
the other three factors are to be mixed.

Factoring
A way for a business to stretch its finances. The factoring
company, or factor, assesses the client firm's flow of
invoices to its own trading customers. Depending on how
good a risk those invoices are, the factor will lend a
proportion to the client immediately, so that he does not
have to wait three months or so. A factor, which may be
owned by one of the big banks, may be in a better position
to lean on a big customer of a small firm. Actual collection
of bad debts is, however, a separate service. Ask your bank
manager.

Fair rent
Dating from the 1965 Rent Act, a fair rent is one set by the
rent officer of a county or county borough. He is called in

whenever landlord and tenant cannot agree on the rent. This system replaced the former controlled rents. See also *Assured tenancy*, *Regulated tenancy*, *Shorthold tenancy*, *Tenant*.

Family income benefit
This is a form of *Life insurance*, aimed at the situation where the death of the breadwinner could leave the other parent to bring up young children for several years. It works on the same basis as *Term assurance*, except that the payout is in instalments instead of a lump sum. This can make it a cheaper form of insurance, because the insurer earns interest on the money he keeps back. It is best suited to a family where the surviving parent has neither the wit nor the inclination to manage a lump sum unaided. The duration and frequency of the payments can be varied, and most insurers will offer an index-linked option. A typical contract sends a monthly cheque for 10 years.

Family income supplement
This is a social security payment to poorer families, where at least one parent is working. It is paid if the family income is below a certain level, excluding child benefit and other allowances. The level is raised for each extra child. Families receiving the supplement are also entitled to free school meals, free dental treatment, medical prescriptions and spectacles, and free milk for under fives and pregnant women.

Federation of Private Residents' Associations
A private organisation which can help you to set up a residents' association, or give advice on disputes with landlords. Its address is 11 Dartmouth Street, London SW1.

Fen
The humblest unit of currency in China. There are 10 fen to a jiao and 100 to a yuan.

Feu duty

Under Scottish law, this is an ancient form of *Ground rent* on property. A feu is a land tenure originally paid for in grain. The system is being phased out: the Tenure Reform (Scotland) Act 1974 prevents the creation of new feu duties and cancels existing ones when land is sold.

FFI See *Investors in Industry*.

Fidelity bond

A bond taken out by an employer to insure against a cashier walking off with the firm's money. The insurer pays only after the thief has been convicted by a court. See *Defalcation*, *Embezzlement*.

Fill or kill

This is a type of order given by an investor in a *Futures* market to his broker. It has to be put to the market three times: if no one deals, the order is immediately cancelled. It is an order which is given when someone wants to take advantage of a rapidly-moving situation. See *Day order*, *Good till cancelled*, *Limit order*, *Market order*.

Final account

This is the finished version of a firm's profit-and-loss account. From it the *Balance sheet* is worked out. See *Bookkeeping*, *Trading account*, *Trial balance*.

Finance

People tend to forget the significance of the 'final' part of finance. Coming, like several other business words, from Old French, 'finance' used to refer to the settling of a debt. It has gradually become widened to take in lending, monetary resources and the whole area of money management.

Finance Act

The final crystallisation of the *Budget* proposals, after they

have been approved by Parliament. It usually appears late
in the summer, after MPs have had a few months to chew
it over. The changes from the original, however, are normally
small and insigificant if the ruling political party has a safe
majority in the House of Commons. The House of Lords is
prevented from delaying a *Finance Bill*.

Finance Bill

The legal form of the measures proposed in the Budget.
Like any other Bill, it then has to be debated and approved
by Parliament before the measures can come into effect
through a Finance Act some months later. However, the
Chancellor can order changes to take place on the day of his
speech, subject to change later. In practice, they rarely are
changed.

Finance for Industry See *Investors in industry*.

Finance house

Finance houses are registered as *Licensed deposit-takers* by
the *Bank of England*. Several of the biggest are owned by
the *Clearing banks*, who regard them as highly profitable
businesses. That means, dear borrower, that they are likely
to charge you more for a loan than the banks themselves do.
On the other hand, finance houses will lend to people who
probably could not get a bank loan. Their speciality is *Hire
purchase*, but they also do *Leasing* and most of them offer
savings schemes too.

Financial Institutions, Report into Workings of See *Wilson Report*.

Financial instrument

This is any stock, share, currency or money. It could be a
Treasury bill, a French franc, a *Gilt-edged* stock, a *Certificate
of deposit*, or any of an infinite number of other securities.
Some of these instruments are dealt in on *Futures* markets.

Financial Times
A daily newspaper covering the whole business spectrum
from economics through to personal finance, including reports
of announcements by just about every quoted company. It
is owned by the publishers, Pearson Longman, which in
turn is part of Pearson. See *FT Index*.

Fine trade bills See *Bills of Exchange*.

Firm
In the financial world, firm can be a noun or an adjective.
A firm is another word for a *Partnership*, and it is often
loosely extended to refer to *Companies*. Firm is also used to
describe market prices if they are rising steadily.

First notice day
This is the first day on which a *Delivery notice* can be sent
to the buyer of a *Futures contract*.

Fiscal
The Latin word *fiscum*, meaning a wicker basket, came to
suggest a purse, and Emperor Augustus used it to refer to
his Treasury. As so often happens, the money tag took over,
and by the 1860s 'fiscal' became a general word for
anything financial. See *Fiscal year*.

Fiscal year
In Britain there are two types of fiscal year. For individuals,
the *Income tax* year runs from April 6 to the following
April 5. But companies pay *Corporation tax* on the basis of
a year running from April 1 to the next March 31.

Fit for Work Campaign
A *Manpower Services Commission* venture aimed at
encouraging employers to take on more disabled people,
and preparing the disabled for work. Disabled people can
also attend the MSC's *TOPS* courses. The Fit for Work
Award Scheme selects employers who are judged to have

been constructive and adopted the most effective policies towards the disabled.

Flat rate
This is the crude measure of interest on an instalment loan. If you borrow £100 for a year and pay £10 interest, that is 10% interest – so long as you have the £100 for the whole year. But if you repay it in instalments, you have not had the use of the loan for the whole time, so your true rate of interest is higher. On equal instalments the true rate works out at nearly double the nominal – or flat – rate. See *Annual percentage rate*, *True rate*.

Flat yield
This is the *Yield* from a fixed interest stock, taking no account of any gain that may be made on the value of the stock itself. See *Redemption yield*.

Flotation
When a company's shares are quoted for the first time on the stock market. This is known as a flotation, from the idea that the firm's backers are floating the shares on the market, which will be expected to keep them bobbing along on the surface. This does not always happen, but every new company at least begins its life on a tide of optimism.

F.o.b.
Free on board. If you import goods F.o.b., that means that you have to pay for insurance and shipping charges. See *C.i.f.*

Folio number
Bookkeeping entries should always be marked with a folio number to show where the other half of the *Double-entry bookkeeping* entry is. See Bookkeeping.

Forint
The forint is the Hungarian currency, with about 60 to the pound.

Franc

Second to the dollar as the world's most popular currency
name. It divides into two main variations, with several
individual brands littered round the globe. Tied to the
French rate of around 12 francs to the pound are the
currencies of French Guiana, Guadaloupe, Monaco,
Reúnion Island in the Pacific, and St Pierre and Miquelon,
off Canada. The second major group of franc nations are
those which form the French Community in Africa, whose
version changes hands at more than 500 to the pound. This
includes the Central African Republic, Comoro Islands,
Congo, Equatorial Guinea, Gabon, Ivory Coast, Malagasy
Republic, Mali, Martinique, Niger Republic, Senegal, Togo
Republic and Upper-Volta.

Off on their own are Djibouti, at the southern end of the
Red Sea, with a franc running at 300 to the pound,
Luxembourg at 80 and Switzerland at about 2.8.
Liechtenstein follows the Swiss rate, and Andorra – on the
border of France and Spain – takes both the franc and the
peseta. See *Cent*.

Franchise

A franchise is a form of freedom. In the commercial world
it has come to mean a freedom granted by a company for
other people to use a trading name or system, usually with
exclusive rights within an agreed territory. This practice
was developed in the United States, but is now widespread
in Britain. It works best when a company has a strong
brand name, well known to the public, and can turn its
business into an easily taught pattern for franchisees to follow.
The franchisee normally pays a fee plus a royalty based on
a percentage of turnover. See *British Franchise Association*.

Franked income

Dividends which a company pays to another company. As
the money has already been subject to *Corporation tax*
once, no more corporation tax has to be paid on it by the
receiving company. See *Gross Funds*.

Free ports
These are ports (sea or air) which are designated by the
Government as free of customs duty, agricultural levies or
European Community duties. The aim is to encourage
re-export business, where goods are imported only so that
they can be made up and exported.

Friedman, Professor Milton
Born New York, 31 July 1912. Major exponent of *Monetarist*
economics. Educated at Rutgers, Chicago and Columbia
universities, awarded a PhD by Columbia. In 1938 married
Rose Director; one son, one daughter. Awarded the Nobel
Memorial Prize for Economics, 1976. Recent publications:
There's No Such Thing as a Free Lunch, 1975; *Price Theory*,
1976; *Free to Choose*, 1980; *Tyranny of the Status Quo*, 1984.
Address: Hoover Institution, Stanford, California, 94305,
USA.

Friendly Societies
A peculiarly British invention, the friendly society first
appeared in the eighteenth century, in an attempt to combat
the financial fears of workers in the early industrial
revolution. Friendly Societies go all the way from Building
Societies to Trades Unions, with thousands of little sickness
and burial clubs in between. The thread running through
them is that all the members put money in, which is drawn
out when they are in need under the rules of each society.
They are monitored by the Chief Registrar of Friendly
Societies, who was created in 1846. His address is 15–17
Great Marlborough Street, London W1V 2AX.

Front-end loading
In most consumer instalment contracts – mortgages, hire
purchase, insurance policies and so on – the lender or
insurer's first concern is to cover his overheads and the cost
of paperwork and staff time. So if you try to end any of
these contracts early, you will usually find that the company
makes a deduction for those costs. This is front-end loading.

It can mean that you will get nothing back if you try to wind up the plan within a year or two. It is a good idea to check this before you sign anything.

FT Index
This index is published hourly by the *Financial Times* and is widely regarded as the barometer of the London stock market. It is based on the share prices of 30 major industrial companies, but does not include *Gilts*. It started in 1935 at a level of 100. Each of the 30 shares is calculated against its own base price on that date. This is done by adding up the logarithms of each one, subtracting an adjusted base figure, dividing the result by 30 and taking the anti-logarithm of that. The FT also has a range of indices covering different industries, and an 'all-share' index begun in 1962.

FT-SE Index
Nicknamed the Footsie index, this is an index of the share prices of the 100 biggest companies on the Stock Exchange. Within the professional investment community it is more popular than the FT 30-share index as it is more representative of the market as a whole – and is big enough for fund managers to use it as the basis of their portfolios.

Funds in court
This is usually money which has been awarded as damages arising out of a civil court case. But if the person receiving the money is too young or too daft to handle it, the court can have it managed for him or her. The Public Trustee takes the responsibility. It is a valuable safety net, but the Public Trustee's investment record has not always been the best in the world.

Futures
This refers to a series of markets, mainly in *Commodities*, foreign exchange and *Bullion*, where a price is fixed today although the goods are not to be delivered for several

months. It is a fertile ground for speculators who think they
can see prices moving one way or another. But it is also a
valuable facility for manufacturers to insure the future
cost of their raw materials. See also *Hedging*, *Spot*, *Traded
option*.

Futures contract
This is a commitment to deliver or receive a *Financial
instrument* at a fixed price and amount, at an agreed future
date. To meet the contract, the instrument must be a
Deliverable name. See *Open contract*.

Gamblers Anonymous
The betting bug can become as addictive as alcohol or any
other drug. By the time a sufferer has got to that stage, it
will be well-nigh impossible to discuss it objectively with
family or close friends. A solution is Gamblers
Anonymous, which works on the lines of Alcoholics
Anonymous. The address is 17 Blantyre Street, London
SW10; tel. 01-352 3060.

GATT See *General Agreement on Tariffs and Trade*.

Gazumping
A slang word born of the early 1970s property boom. Prices
then were rising so quickly that some house sellers were
agreeing a price with one would-be buyer and then welshing
on the deal if someone else made a higher offer. That is
gazumping. This was possible because, under English law,
neither side is committed to a property deal until the
contract is signed. Scottish law is stricter.

Gearing
Gearing is the ratio between the amount of *Shareholders'
funds* in a company and the amount of money borrowed
by that company. The more a company has borrowed, the
more highly it is geared. As in a car, high gearing means
two things: you can go faster, and if you go too fast you will

crash. The reason is that interest on loans has to be paid
before dividends on the shares. If a company has to pay
interest of £1m a year, until it has made enough profit to
clear that, shareholders can get nothing. But if the business
makes good use of the loans for expansion, then once profits
are over £1m the return to shareholders rises very quickly.
So gearing is riskier, but potentially more rewarding. In the
US it is called *Leverage*.

General Agreement on Tariffs and Trade
An international agreement signed in 1947 with the aim of
reducing worldwide tariff barriers. Because its remit is so
wide it has had limited direct effect. But it is the only global
forum for world trade, and every few years a determined
effort is made to use its mechanism to cut tariffs. A notable
example was the Kennedy round in the early 1960s.

General Agreement to Borrow
This is an agreement between the *International Monetary
Fund* and the *Group of Ten*. It allows the IMF to supplement
its own resources with extra loans from the countries
belonging to the Group of Ten, all of whom are also
members of the IMF. The GAB amounts to an emergency
fund.

General Commissioners
These are members of the public who hear appeals by
taxpayers against tax assessments by the Inspectors of
Taxes. They are unpaid, can be up to 75 years old, and
employ a clerk as legal adviser and to handle paper work.
Taxpayers can instead choose to be heard by the *Special
Commissioners*. In Northern Ireland the system works
through the County Court. See also *Commissioners of Inland
Revenue*.

General legacy
A *Legacy* of a straightforward cash sum, like £500. It can
also be called a *Pecuniary legacy*.

Gilts

Jargon for British Government stocks. These are notes issued by the government in return for loans and are, in effect, a promise to repay. They became known as gilt-edged after the UK Treasury won a name for paying its debts on time – unlike some of the more obscure countries who came to London to raise money. Gilts, like most other loan stocks, carry the right to a dividend every half-year until the end of their life, when holders are repaid £100 for every unit, no matter how much they originally paid. But make sure there is a set date for repayment. Undated gilts have a less than gilt-edged record.

Girobank

A government-run banking network operating through the 22,000 Post Office branches in Britain. It works like a bank, except that borrowing from it can be more difficult, it does not issue credit cards and you cannot get financial advice. But it issues chequebooks, you can have your wages or salary paid into it, and there is a transfer system between Giro account holders. The Post Offices are also open longer hours than banks.

Gold See *Bullion*.

Gold standard

In its purest form, as it operated in Britain until 1914, putting a currency on the gold standard means that it is freely swoppable into gold and its value is stated in terms of gold. Until 1914 the British sovereign was worth 123.27447 grains of 22-carat gold. When an economy is as powerful as Britain's was in the Victorian era, it can easily maintain a gold standard. But in time of trouble, it ties government's hands. So we came off it when gold was needed for the war effort. Britain returned to it in a diluted form between 1925 and 1931, but was forced off it again because of soaring imports and unemployment. The US dollar was on the gold standard between 1944 and 1971. See *Bretton Woods*.

Golden handshake, Golden parachute See *Compensation for Loss of Office*.

Good till cancelled
On a *Futures* market, this is a type of order by an investor, telling the broker that it stands until it is fulfilled or cancelled. It is usually cancelled automatically at the end of the *Last trading day* for that *Futures contract*. See *Day order, Fill or kill, Limit order, Market order*.

Goodwill
At best, a highly nebulous notion in the business world, at worst a ghost. It springs into balance sheets when a company has taken over another concern at a price higher than the value of that firm's assets. The new assets bed into the combined balance sheet quite easily. But the shares or loans which have been created on the liabilities side of the balance sheet have to find a partner among the assets, and the answer is to put the extra under goodwill. It can stand for the energy, know-how and contacts brought in by the staff of the firm that has been bought. But that soon becomes harder to pick out as time goes on, and it is something you cannot rely on selling. So auditors usually lobby the group's directors to write it out after a year or two.

Gourde
Haiti's currency unit, worth about 15p.

Government broker
Until 1984, the Bank of England bought and sold Gilts through a specially appointed stockbroker, Mullen & Co. But when Mullens agreed to merge with Mercury Securities, the Bank took the opportunity to end this arrangement ahead of the reforms in the gilt market being introduced in 1986.

Graduated pension See *Earnings related pension*.

Granny bond See *Index-linked certificate*.

Grant
This can be either a noun or a verb. To grant something is to give or allow it, and what is granted is often called a grant. In everyday use, a grant is something which is given without usually expecting anything in return, like a gift. It is used in law when something is permitted, such a grant of *Probate*.

Grant redemption fund
When a *Housing association* builds some homes, it usually needs a *Housing association grant* to meet the cost of the land and building work. This is worked out in relation to the *Fair rent* at that time. But rents tend to rise, while the land and building costs are fixed. So housing associations must keep a grant redemption fund, consisting of the extra cash from the higher rents, after paying for repairs and administration.

Green card
An essential if you are taking your own car abroad. Your motor insurer will send you one on request, and it acts as an international certificate to prove that you are covered. As the European Community's insurance laws become more harmonised, the green card should become less vital. But for the foreseeable future it will remain a valuable financial passport for anyone whose car is wrecked in a foreign land.

Green form scheme
This is a way of getting free legal advice for people whose income is below a certain level. It also covers aid on a restricted list of court proceedings. The local *Citizens' Advice Bureau* or legal advice centre can help.

Green pound
This is a European Community invention used to decide

prices under the *Common Agricultural Policy*. The
bureaucrats take the various national currencies out of the
free marketplace and fix their values, moving them only
after lengthy negotiation. The stronger the green pound,
the cheaper our dairy produce but the less our farmers are
paid. The green pound is also part of the *European Currency
Unit*.

Gresham's Law

'Bad money drives out good' is the catchphrase of this
theory. It points out that if a superior money material, such
as gold or silver, is replaced by something inferior like nickel
or paper, people will use the new and hoard the old. Sir
Thomas Gresham was a financier who advised Elizabeth I,
and he had seen this sort of thing happening in Henry
VIII's reign. Some sources claim that Oresme was first with
the theory, in France 200 years before Gresham. People
still hoard gold sovereigns today.

Groschen

A German currency term, dating back to 1613 and connected
to the French word gros. It has long been abandoned by
Germany, but is used in Austria as a hundredth of a schilling.
It is somewhat academic, though, as a schilling is worth
only about 3p.

Gross

Outside the financial world, gross means thick, heavy,
overweight. But in the sixteenth century it became used in
business in contrast to *Net*. The gross amount of a weight
or sum of money is the whole lot, without any deductions.
When deductions have been made, the result is the net
amount.

Gross current replacement cost

The cost of buying a new replacement for an asset a business
is already using. See *Net replacement cost, Replacement cost*.

Gross fund
A pool of money which is exempt from having to make
direct payments of *Capital gains tax* or *Income Tax*. The
capital gains laws contain a list of exempt 'persons', as it
insists on calling them. They include charities, friendly
societies, most pension funds, trade unions, housing
associations, UK local authorities, agricultural societies,
scientific research associations and some government bodies.
Such groups tend not to pay income tax, because they
receive dividends ranking as *Franked income*.

Gross profit See *Trading account*.

Gross value
The gross value of a property is the yearly rent which a
landlord ought to be able to charge, as gauged by a local
council. This is used as the basis of *Rent pooling* and of
working out the *Rateable value* of each property.

Ground rent
Rent on the ground on which a building stands, as opposed
to rent on the occupancy of the building itself. In English
law, it is charged by a freeholder who sells a lease on a
property, to establish the landlord–tenant relationship.

Group
A group is a number of different items which, when brought
together, form a collective unit. In corporate terms, a group
of companies consists of a *Holding company* and its
subsidiaries.

Group of Ten
The ten in question are the West's top ten industrial nations:
Belgium, Britain, Canada, France, Germany, Italy, Japan,
Netherlands, Sweden and the United States. Their finance
ministers and senior finance ministry civil servants meet
from time to time to discuss world money matters. It has
been able to organise rescue packages for countries in
difficulties. See also *General Agreement to Borrow*.

GTC See *Good till cancelled*.

Guaraní
Like most of the south American currencies, the Paraguayan guaraní is fairly volatile, running at around 500 to the pound. Named after a local tribe, the guaraní replaced the peso in 1943.

Guarantee
Can be either a verb or a noun. It involves giving someone else a promise that a debt will be honoured, or that a service will be performed faithfully, or that goods sold will match what the customer paid for. Under the Supply of Goods (Implied Terms) Act, a shopkeeper's or maker's guarantee cannot take away the buyer's legal rights: it can only add to them. Guarantee has become synonymous with warranty, or the verb to warrant.

Guaranteed bonds
These are insurance schemes based on single-premium with-profit endowment contracts running from three to ten years. What is guaranteed is a minimum level of annual bonuses, which you agree to at the outset. These bonuses are then paid out year by year as a form of income to you, or you can opt for guaranteed growth bonds where the bonuses are ploughed back to earn interest and you get a bigger lump sum at the end. Both types are free of basic rate income tax and capital gains tax. They are not to be confused with the earlier type of guaranteed income bonds, which escaped higher rates of tax but were outlawed by the Inland Revenue in 1981.

Guaranteed minimum pension See *Contracting out*.

Guarantor
You may find yourself being asked by a friend or neighbour to act as a guarantor on a *Hire purchase* contract they are taking out. Think hard before you agree. Guarantors become legally

liable for the remaining debt if the borrower cannot keep up the instalments – and you cannot pull out of the guarantee, even if you run out of cash yourself.

Guardian's allowance
This is a payment in addition to *Child benefit* for anyone who is giving a home to a child orphaned because of the death of both parents or the death of a divorced parent who had custody, or because one parent has died and the other is either missing or in prison for at least five years. Ironically, this tax-free payment does not apply if the guardian has legally adopted the child.

Guilder
Derived from the old Dutch word for 'golden', the guilder is the currency of the Netherlands. The name has been lent to the currencies of Surinam (the former Netherlands Guinea) in South America, and of the islands which form the Netherlands Antilles off the coast of Venezuela. The Dutch guilder is worth about 20p, while the Antilles and Surinam version costs about 45p.

Hammering
This is the formal announcement on the floor of the Stock Exchange to tell the members that one of their number has gone bust. It is important that everyone knows at once, so that they can avoid doing any more business with that member or firm. To attract attention, a hammer used to be banged. Today, though, a bell is used.

Hao
The middle currency unit of Vietnam. There are 10 hao to the Vietnamese dong, and the hao is itself divided into 10 xu.

Hard currency
A national currency which has a stable or rising value in foreign exchange markets. It is usually based on a strong *Balance of payments*, or some strong mineral wealth, such as

gold, diamonds or oil – though even these may not be enough if a country has deep-seated problems, such as political instability. The hardness of the currency is a tribute to its ability to withstand bouts of selling by currency dealers. Once that feeling sets in, selling by speculators tends to dry up anyway.

Head and shoulders
A trend on a share-price *Chart* which traces the shape of a head and shoulders. It can mean that a share price has peaked out and is heading downwards. It is even more convincing if it does this twice at about the same level – known to the cognoscenti as a double top. A reverse head-and-shoulders produces the same shape, but upside down, and can be read as a signal to buy the share in question.

Hedging
This is a technique used on *Futures* markets. A trader can protect himself against loss by buying *Spot* and selling at the price currently quoted for future delivery, or vice versa. This limits his losses or profits.

Help the Aged
An organisation which aims both to help old people and to improve their rights. Its address is 1 Sekforde Street, London EC1R 0BE. See also *Age Concern*, *Employment Fellowship* and the *Pre-Retirement Association of Great Britain and Northern Ireland*.

High/low indicator
Like the *Advance/decline line*, this is a *Chartist* weapon for deciding whether the main share indices are telling the full story about the market. It shows the number of shares reaching new high or low prices over a period. When this is going against the index trend, it can indicate a change in the market's direction.

Hire
If you pay to borrow something, intending to return it, you

are hiring it. Americans extend the idea to borrowing a
person's effort, in hiring labour. A variation on the theme
is *Hire purchase.*

Hire purchase

Although HP is generally seen as a way of borrowing money,
what you are really borrowing are the goods you want to buy.
Strictly speaking, you are only hiring them until you have
paid the last instalment, and legally you cannot sell them
until then. But to the borrower the distinction matters little.
You sign a contract agreeing to pay so much a month for
a set period, usually between one and five years. The longer
you can spread the instalments, the less each instalment
will be. But of course over a longer period you will end up
paying more interest, which can be quite high if you work
it out as an *Annual percentage rate.* But what concerns most
people when they want a car or a fridge, or a cooker, is whether
they can afford the monthly commitment. And when prices
are rising fast, it can make sense to buy on HP now rather
than saving up first.

Holding company

A company whose main business consists in holding shares
or other types of security in subsidiaries where the holding
company has at least 75% in each case. See *Group.*

Home income plan

This is a type of scheme for old people to squeeze an income
out of their home. If you are 70 or over you can take out a
Mortgage on your house and use the money to buy an
Annuity, which pays a regular sum back to you. Abbey
National Building Society operates such a plan, and so do
some insurance firms. *The British Insurance Association* will
give an up-to-date list.

Home-loan scheme

This is a government scheme designed to help first-time
house buyers. If you save for at least two years in a savings

account opened with a member of the scheme, and build up more than a laid-down minimum sum, you will get a cash bonus. Building societies, banks and the National Savings Department all operate the scheme: make sure you fill in the special form when you open an account with one of them.

Home responsibilities protection

Someone who looks after a child, or a sick or elderly person, can be given exemption from paying National Insurance contributions. The years in which the protection is granted count in full towards the pension of the person doing the caring. Ask your local Social Security office for details.

Home service insurance

This is the door-to-door system of collecting insurance, typified by the *Man from the Pru*. It used to be called industrial insurance, because it originated in industrial areas where people could afford only a weekly premium and preferred the personal contact with an agent who would also be a salesman. Two out of every three doors feel the weekly knock from the insurance man.

Hospital treatment allowance

A top-up payment under the *Disablement benefit* scheme. If a victim is rated at less than 100% disability, this allowance brings them up to the 100% level of benefit while they are hospital in-patients. See also *Constant attendance allowance*.

Hot money

This is money which hurtles from country to country, chasing the hardest currency and the highest interest rates. It is called hot because if enough of it lands in the same place at once it can create havoc with the local currency – and it can vanish just as quickly. Hot money is most likely to surface when international currencies are in a state of flux and no one is sure which chair will be removed when the music stops. In quieter times, it all cools down. See *Eurodollars*

Household insurance
Although the phrase is self-explanatory, it is important to remember that household insurance divides into two broad categories: building and contents. The first refers to the cost of repairing damage to the structure of a house, up to and including complete rebuilding. Contents insurance covers loss of or damage to furniture, carpets, curtains and personal belongings. This can be extended to protect valuables taken outside the house. Household insurance is a cheap way of shrinking a lot of worries, but a quarter of houses are not covered because people think it is not going to happen to them. But it does.

Housekeeper allowance
If you are widowed, you can claim this tax allowance if you have a housekeeper – even a relative – living in your home. If the housekeeper is related, though, this allowance cannot be claimed if her husband is collecting the *Married man's allowance*. And if you still have a child at home it is better to claim the *Additional allowance for children*.

Housing association
This is a private organisation, often set up with money from a charity, which aims to provide housing at low rents. Guinness and Peabody are two of the most well-known. Shelter, the national campaign for the homeless, has raised several million pounds to start housing associations. The *Housing corporation* can help, too.

Housing association grant
This is a grant to help *Housing associations* to build homes. When a *Fair rent* has been fixed on a new home, the association must work out how far that rent will pay for repairs, administration and the cost of servicing a loan to cover the

price of the land and building work. If it falls short, the association calculates how big a loan it will service. The grant is designed to meet some or all of the rest of the capital cost. If not, the association may then have to apply to the local council or the *Housing corporation*. See also *Grant redemption fund*, *Revenue deficit subsidy*.

Housing benefit
This is a scheme to bring the present housing allowances into one. It would replace rent and rate rebates, rent allowances and supplementary benefits, and help with housing costs.

Housing capital account
This is an account kept by local councils. It shows on one side what has been spent on land, sewers, roads and the buildings themselves. The other side shows loans raised to pay for the spending. See also *Housing revenue account*.

Housing Corporation
A government-backed body which keeps an eye on *Housing associations*, lends money on do-it-yourself building schemes, and puts interested people in touch with one another. It also publishes helpful books. There are regional offices, and the head office is at Maple House, 149 Tottenham Court Road, London W1P 0BN.

Housing grants
These are given by local authorities to encourage householders to keep their homes up to scratch. In most cases they are subject to the council's own financial position, so they may be available only for a limited period. But if you are thinking of spending money on your home, it is always worth a call to ask what grants are to be had at that time. See *Improvement grant*, *Repair grant*, *Special grant*.

Housing investment programme
This is a form sent by each local council each year to the
Department of the Environment, showing how much money
it wants to spend on the various projects outlined in its *Local
housing strategy*. The government then decides how much
it can afford overall, and hands the money out accordingly.
But if the government subsequently decides that a
particular scheme will give 'exceptionally poor value', it can
refuse the usual subsidy.

Housing revenue account
This is an account kept by local councils to show the costs
of running the houses it provides. The income side consists
of rent less rebates, housing subsidies and other grants from
the government. The money is spent on paying interest
on loans needed to build the houses, repayment of those
loans, repairs and management. See *Housing capital
account*.

ICFC See *Industrial and Commercial Finance Corporation,
Investors In Industry*.

IMF See *International Monetary Fund*.

Imperfect competition
That untidy but common state lying between the two
economic myths of *Perfect competition* and *Monopoly*.

Imprest
An advance of money needed to enable an employee to do
a job. Typically, a junior cashier will be given an imprest for
the petty cash box. It may be £50. As the money is handed
out, it is regularly topped up to the imprest level. Imprest
also used to be the word for money to pay soldiers and
sailors, and it can still refer to an advance by the government
to pay for a particular project.

Improvement grant
This is perhaps the most widespread type of *Housing grant*

offered by local authorities. The terms will vary between
different councils and different periods, but they will often
pay at least half the cost of building an extension, rewiring,
installing a damp course or power points, or repointing. See
Housing grants, *Repair grant*, *Special grant*.

Imputation tax

A horror of a tax, introduced in 1973 to refine the *Corporation
tax* system to make it easier to pay dividends. Dividends are
liable to income tax. When shareholders receive their
cheques, the tax is 'imputed' or credited to the company's
own tax bill by paying the Inland Revenue an instalment of
Advance Corporation Tax. When the firm's corporation
tax is eventually calculated, anything still to be paid after
deducting ACT is called mainstream corporation tax. This
hits UK businesses with major interests overseas, as ACT
cannot be offset against foreign profit. The system inhibits
dividend payments, as the higher the dividend, the sooner
a company pays tax – in the form of ACT.

In specie See *Specie*.

Income

The money you receive regularly, mainly from the work you
do or the investments you own. That, at least, is the sort
of income the Inland Revenue is interested in when it is
deciding how much to tax you. It may be boosted
occasionally by a pools win or a legacy from Aunt Jemima.
But the taxman ignores gambling winnings and will look
at an inheritance only if it might involve *Inheritance Tax*. A
grey area is the profit made on selling investments. Normally
they are liable to *Capital Gains Tax*. But if you make money
often in this way you may be regarded as a trader – and made
to pay income tax, a stiffer penalty. The same goes for selling
your home. In most cases, any profit is tax-free. But a
second home can attract gains tax, and if you move too often
you may be put into the property-dealer pigeon-hole.

Income fund

This is a type of *unit trust*. It offers a high yield in the form of regular dividends, rather than promising much capital growth. But if you catch an income fund just before interest rates begin to fall, you can pick up some growth too.

Income tax

The idea of a tax on people's incomes was regarded as a heinous affront to the rights and privacy of the individual when it was introduced by William Pitt in 1799. His excuse was the cost of the Napoleonic Wars, and the tax was abolished in 1816. But it returned in 1842 and is with us to stay as a staple of government revenue. The *Basic rate* is currently 30p in the pound on income over and above the level of *Personal allowances*. There are also higher rates for higher levels of income, up to a maximum of 60%. The bands of income are changed at nearly every *Budget*. See *Inland Revenue, Investment income surcharge, Schedules A to F*.

Incorporated Society of Valuers and Auctioneers

A leading body for estate agents and house surveyors. Its members carry the letters FSVA or ASVA after their name, which should guarantee a minimum standard of professional competence. Its address is 3 Cadogan Gate, London SW1 0AS.

Indemnity

Indemnity is compensation for loss, so that if someone has an insurance policy, we say he is indemnified. It also has a political or legal meaning, when a person is exempted from the penalties which would normally apply on breaking a law.

Independent Schools Information Service

Gives information about private schools round the country. Can also put parents on to sources of finance for *School fees*. The address is National ISIS, 56 Buckingham Gate, London SW1E 6AG.

Indexation See *Index-linking*.

Indexation of allowances See *Personal allowances*.

Indexing See *Index-linking*.

Index-linked certificates
After many years of outcry from savers, in 1975 the National Savings Department eventually came up with an inflation-proof bond. At first it was only available to pensioners, giving rise to the nickname *Granny Bond*. But the age qualification has been gradually lowered – as the rate of inflation also dipped, making these certificates less attractive. See *National Savings Certificates, Premium Bonds, Save As You Earn*.

Index-linked gilts
These are gilts with a relatively small *running yield* which is adjusted for inflation by reference to the retail prices index.

Index-linking
As inflation grew in the 1970s, people tried to protect themselves by demanding that their income be linked to the rise in the *Retail Prices Index*. One of the first examples of index-linking was civil service pensions. Since then many pay rises were, if only unofficially, worked out with an eye on the index and the government eventually issued index-linked bonds.

Indirect tax
A tax which is paid to the government through another medium, usually when goods or services are bought. It includes *Customs and Excise Duties* and *Value Added Tax*. See also *Direct tax*.

Industrial and Commercial Finance Corporation
A subsidiary of *Investors in Industry*, which in turn is owned by the *Bank of England* and the major *Clearing banks*,

ICFC is designed to channel money into up-and-coming businesses and new industries. As such, it has also become an excellent information exchange on what is happening at knee level in the business world. It does not tend to invest in pure start-up situations. It is based at 91 Waterloo Road, London SE1, but has offices round the country. See *Equity capital for industry*.

Industrial and Provident Society
This is a society registered under the Industrial and Provident Societies Act 1965, or the Industrial and Provident Societies Act (Northern Ireland) 1969. For tax purposes, share dividends or bonuses and loan interest paid by such a society is not treated as a *Distribution*. Instead, it can set such payments against its trading income. But the society must tell the Inland Revenue the name and address of everyone to whom it has paid more than £15 in a year.

Industrial death
The dependents of someone who has died through an industrial injury or *Disease* can claim benefit from their local social security office. Widows can collect benefit unless and until they remarry. Extra is paid for children. A widower can claim if he had been unable to support himself and his wife had been paying more than half the cost of keeping him. Other relatives can claim under special circumstances. Check with the local *Social Security* office, or *Citizens' Advice Bureau*.

Industrial insurance See *Home service insurance*.

Industrial Language Training Service
Run by the *Manpower Services Commission*, this service is designed to help those whose first language is not English, so that they can fare better at work. It is also aimed at managers and trades unionists who deal with people from ethnic minorities. Local education authorities provide staff for Industrial Language Training Units. Overall advice on the

service comes from the National Centre for Industrial
Language Training.

Industrial Reorganisation Corporation See *British
Technology Group*.

Industrial Tribunal
This is a three-person committee set up to hear complaints
from workers who have been sacked from or denied a job,
and from employers who feel they have been unfairly treated
by the Department of Employment. It consists of a lawyer
chairman, and a member each nominated by employers and
the unions. You apply to the tribunal on Form ITI, from your
shop steward, Job Centre or unemployment office. In most
cases you have to apply within three months. Check with
your union or *Citizens' Advice Bureau* as to whether you
have a case. See also *Conciliation officer*.

Industry
Industry still retains the range of meanings it acquired in
the first 50 years after it passed into common usage in
1566, from diligence and hard or determined work, through
to the production of goods to sell. It became more sharply
defined in the Victorian era, when the industrial revolution
brought clanking machinery and dark satanic mills to the
centre of the stage. Nowadays, it can refer to one specific
industry – even in services such as advertising or life
insurance – or to industry as a whole, as in the *Confederation
of British Industry*.

Inelasticity See *Elasticity*.

Inflation
This puts money through a distorting mirror of constantly
rising wages and prices. It makes it harder to see how
expensive goods really are – and how much your income
and savings are really worth.

Inheritance Tax

This is Capital Transfer Tax by another name, as retitled in
the 1986 Budget. Unlike the old CTT, it excludes most
outright gifts by a living person and so reverts to something
very like the old Death Duty. The tax begins to bite seven
years before the giver dies, then rises progressively in order
to prevent deathbed gifts escaping the net.

Initial allowance

When a business has spent money on an asset, part of it can
be offset against tax. But since 1970 it has not applied to
plant and machinery, which since then has been covered by
the *First-year allowance*. See *Balancing allowance*,
Writing-down allowance. In 1984 it was abolished for
everything except business building, enterprise zones and
scientific research.

Initial margin

This is a deposit which an investor on a *Futures* market must
put down when he enters a *Futures contract*. It is worked out
as a proportion of the value of that contract. See *Eligible
margin*, *Maintenance margin*, *Variation margin*.

Injury benefit

An alternative to *Sickness benefit* for employees who cannot
work because of an accident or disease caused at work. It
is paid instead of sickness benefit, *Unemployment benefit*,
Invalidity or *Retirement pension*, *Maternity allowance* or
Widow's benefit, so it is worth checking which pays most.
After 26 weeks the victim is entitled to *Disablement benefit*,
which is paid in addition to sickness benefit. See also *Disease*.

Inland Revenue

The government department responsible for deciding how
much tax people and companies should pay, and collecting it.
However, *Value-Added Tax*, *Excise duty* and *Customs duty*
on imports are handled by the *Customs and Excise
Department*. See also *Commissioners of Inland Revenue*.

Inland Revenue Tribunal
A judicial body which looks at attempts to stop tax avoidance on dealings in stocks and shares, decides how much tax non-residents should pay and can be asked to review the tax reliefs on wear and tear of machinery.

Input tax See *Value-Added Tax.*

Insider dealing
Insiders are people inside or close to a company whose shares are quoted on the stock market. They include directors, their secretaries and senior executives, and the company's financial advisers – auditors, lawyers, bankers, stockbrokers, public relations consultants. Under the 1980 Companies Act, if any of these people trade in the company's shares – or pass information enabling someone else to do so – on the basis of confidential information, they have broken the law. Given the secret nature of the offence, it has been difficult to prove cases of insider dealing. But it has at least made directors more careful.

Insolvent
Unable to meet financial obligations – particularly if you cannot pay your debts. It is the same as being *Bankrupt*, but it can also be applied to companies. See *Solvent.*

Inspector of Taxes
Commissioners of Inland Revenue appoint civil servants as inspectors to issue and inspect *Tax return* forms so as to decide how much *Income tax* people should pay. Anyone with a tax problem should write to his local inspector of taxes. Their addresses are in the phone book. See also *Collector of Taxes.*

Institute of Chartered Accountants in England and Wales
The main accountancy body in Great Britain. It lays down standards of both training and practice for the profession. Fully qualified members of the Institute become Fellows

and are allowed to put the letters FCA after their name.
The Institute is at Moorgate Place, London EC2. There is
a separate Institute of Chartered Accountants of Scotland,
at 27 Queen Street, Edinburgh EH2 1LA.

Institute of Directors

This is the main body representing company directors in
Britain. It acts as a pressure group, lobbying government
on tax changes and economic policy. It is complementary to
the *Confederation of British Industry*, which represents the
companies themselves. The Institute's address is 116 Pall
Mall, London SW1Y 5ED.

Institute of Personnel Management

This organisation represents personnel managers, and has
been responsible for introducing higher standards through
training courses and different grades of membership. It is
also able to advise people wishing to enter the profession.
Its address is IPM House, 35 Camp Road, London SW19
4VW.

Insurance

Insurance is an attempt to stave off the worst effects of
future misfortune – or at least to make sure you have some
money to drown your sorrows. The insured pays a premium
to the insurer, who promises to pay an agreed sum if a
specified event occurs. It can cover certainties, such as death,
and it can be attached to a form of investment, like a unit
trust. Some insurance is compulsory in Britain, particularly
against injuring others in car accidents. Insurance
resembles betting in that the less likely an occurrence, the
higher the odds or the lower the premium. See *Household
insurance, Life insurance, Motor insurance, Medical insurance,
Travel insurance, Under-insurance, Loss adjuster, Public Loss
Assessor, Comprehensive insurance, Professional indemnity
insurance, Public liability insurance, Weather insurance.*

Insurance agent

If someone knocks on your door or telephones you to sell

insurance, find out who he is working for. A bona fide insurance broker is likely to be independent of any one insurer, and should be able to give objective advice. An agent, however, is probably employed by one or two insurance firms and will be likely to push the policies of those firms – whether or not they are best for your needs.

Insurance Brokers' Registration Council
This is the body responsible for, in effect, licensing insurance brokers. Until a few years ago, anyone who wanted to sell insurance could simply set up shop, subject to the laws of fraud. But now brokers have to show some knowledge and experience of the business. The Council has a professional code of conduct, and a fund to compensate anyone who has been defrauded. Its address is St Helens Place, London EC3.

Insurance-linked building society savings
This is a type of scheme offered by several building societies, designed to take advantage of their own high rates of interest and the tax relief on insurance premiums. The monthly payment pass from you to the society to the insurance firm, which deducts its costs but registers the tax benefit and passes it back to the society to invest the cash in a special account. It is a form of *Endowment* policy linked to a specific but safe investment. There are the usual advantages to younger savers/policyholders, together with the normal benefit if you die early. You have to leave the money in for at least four years. See *Building society, Insurance*.

Insurance Ombudsman Bureau
There are over 20 insurance companies which belong to this bureau, set up to investigate complaints and settle disputes with policyholders. See also *British Insurance Association*.

Inter dealer broker
A stock market firm which handles deals between gilt-edged *market makers*.

Interest
If you are financially interested in something, be it a *Business*, *Enterprise*, *Venture*, ICI shares, that pound you lent last week or the result of the 1.45 at Wincanton, you expect to get some money back – preferably more than you put in. Some interest is fixed, and fairly certain, like the rate of interest on a *Loan*. Some is fixed but pretty uncertain, like the odds on a horse. And some is unknown until it is in the bag, such as a business profit.

Interest cover
A company's profits before any interest or tax payable, divided by the bill for interest on loans. If the interest matches or exceeds the profit, there is obviously nothing left for shareholders, suggesting that the company is borrowing more than it can handle.

Interest yield
Another term for *Running yield*.

International Bank for Reconstruction and Development
See *World Bank*.

International Development Association See *World Bank*.

International Finance Corporation See *World Bank*.

International Monetary Fund
Based in Washington, the US capital, the IMF reports to the United Nations and is backed by most countries in the world. They all contribute an agreed amount of their own currencies and an artificial currency called *Special Drawing Rights*. In turn, the members can ask the IMF for help to see them through short-term *Balance of payments* problems. But if they borrow over a certain amount, the IMF staff flies in to enforce changes in the borrowing government's economic policies. Longer-term lending is carried out by the *World Bank*. See also *Bretton Woods*, *General Agreement to Borrow*.

Intestate
Testari is a Latin word meaning to bear witness or make a
Will. Someone who is intestate has not made a will. If you
die intestate, your property is distributed according to the
intestacy rules laid down by law. If those rules suit your
wishes, or you do not care what happens after your death,
do not make a will. But it is as well to consult a solicitor
or your local *Citizens' Advice Bureau*. The number is in the
phone book.

Introducing member
A stock market firm which acts purely as a broker, leaving
all the paperwork to a *Clearing member*.

Introduction
This is a genteel City of London parlance for a type of share
flotation. A company's stockbrokers get permission for the
shares to be quoted on the Stock Exchange, then sell parcels
of them privately. The market jobbers will buy some to
trade, and the broker's other clients will be offered some.
Then dealings proper begin on the market. This is often
done for small firms, as it costs less in professional fees than
an offer for sale or a tender. Introductions are also chosen
where the brokers do not think the shares are likely to set
the world alight, and might flop with a more public form
of début. The shares usually start quietly, because no one
knows how many the broker will be feeding on to the
market for the next few months.

Invalid care allowance
If you have to give up work to take care of a sick or disabled
relative, you can claim this allowance from your local Social
Security office. It must be a full-time task, the relative must
be near family, and you must be earning next to nothing. Any
other social security benefits you collect will be offset against
this one. Wives living with their husbands cannot claim, but
a man entitled to the allowance can claim extra for his wife,

dependent children, and in some cases a housekeeper. See *Disability benefit, Disabled*.

Invalidity allowance
This is paid in addition to an *Invalidity pension*, to compensate for a shortened career. The biggest allowance is for the under-40s, a smaller amount goes to those between 40 and 49 when first disabled, and a lower rate still for men between 50 and 59, and women between 50 and 54.

Invalidity benefit See *Disability benefit*.

Invalidity pension
This is payable to people unable to work, after their right to *Sickness benefit* has run out. You have to have been disabled for at least 168 days, which can be in separate spells, so long as there is no more than 13 weeks between any two spells. This pension is geared to your *National Insurance* contributions, but there is also a scheme for people whose contributions are too small. Here you must be a UK resident over 16 (19 if still studying), and have lived in the UK for 10 out of the past 20 years, and 26 weeks out of the past year. You must have been disabled for at least 28 weeks. See *Disabled, Invalidity allowance*.

Inverted market
A *Futures* market in which *Futures contracts* in the nearer months are selling for more than those which have several months to go. Usually it is the other way round.

Investment business
Under the Financial Services Act, all investment businesses will have to be authorised by the *Securities and Investments Board*. For the purposes of the Act, an investment business can cover anything from dealing in or advising on investments, to managing them or running a collective investment scheme such as a unit trust.

Investment club
This can be a pleasant way of investing if you do not have
enough money on your own, or simply want to pool ideas.
Against that, of course, it is not for people who do not like
bowing to the wishes of the majority. It is important to
draw up a clear set of rules at the outset, and to keep proper
accounts. Otherwise you get in a muddle. A time limit is
also a good idea, to give people a definite chance to get out.
If the club is going to have more than a few members, it
is worth consulting a solicitor.

Investment consultant
An impressive title – but legally meaningless. Anyone
can call him or herself an investment consultant. No
qualifications are necessary, and there is no specific
trade association. However, investment consultants
may belong to one of the recognised groups, such as
the *British Insurance Brokers Association,* or the *National
Association of Securities Dealers and Investment Managers.*
Otherwise, beware.

Investment trust
A device for small investors to get the advantages of a wide
spread of investments. All the money is put into a pool, which
is then invested by the directors or managers, often in line
with a declared policy such as pursuing high technology
or oil or Japanese shares. It is similar to a *Unit trust,* but
there is a crucial difference. The price of a unit is simply the
value of the trust divided by the number of units, but the
price of a share in an investment trust goes up and down
with stock market demand. So while unit prices are always
equal to the value of the underlying assets, investment
trust shares frequently stand at a discount. But they can rise
a lot faster than units, especially if the directors borrow to
give the fund some *Gearing.* The first investment trust in
England was the Foreign and Colonial Government Trust,
1868.

Investors In Industry
Finance for Industry, renamed Investors in Industry in 1983
and promptly abbreviated to 3i. It is owned by the *Bank
of England* and the *Clearing banks*, and aims to channel
money into industry as one of the City's attempts to bridge
the alleged gap between the bank's lending rules and
deserving causes which might otherwise be overlooked. It was
set up in 1973, and took under its wing the *Industrial and
Commercial Finance Corporation*, which had been operating
since 1945. 3i is in turn a key investor in *Equity Capital for
Industry*.

Invisible exports/imports See *Current account*.

Invoice
A business document describing a *Transaction*. It should
state what goods or services are being sold, their quantity
and price, and the date. The name of the seller will normally
be on the invoice, as he is issuing it, and in trades between
two firms the buyer's name will be recorded too. An invoice
is not a legal document, but it can count as evidence that
a sale contract has been struck. See also *Receipt*.

Issued capital
This is the part of the authorised capital which has actually
been issued, either by selling or through share exchanges
as part of a merger.

Jevons See *Sunspot Theory*.

Jiao
The middle currency unit in China. Called 'mao', there are
10 to the yuan, and the jiao is worth 10 fen.

Job Centre
The unemployed person's job-hunting base. Jobs are
advertised on cards which are classified on boards
according to different types. Each card has a reference

number. If you quote this at one of the Job Centre's staff, they will give you more details and try to get in touch with the employer to arrange the interview.

Job Release Scheme
A State scheme to encourage men aged 62 or more to retire early, to let a younger unemployed person have his job. The 62-year-olds must not get another job, but they receive a weekly taxable allowance. Men over 64 and women over 59 collect a smaller, but tax-free, sum. Both are cut if they have a spouse earning over a given level.

Job Search Scheme
Part of the *Employment Service Division* of the *Manpower Services Commission*, this scheme helps job seekers to go to interviews.

Job splitting
A government scheme to encourage companies to share a job between two people, enabling them to retain workers whom they might otherwise have to let go. Or a firm may be able to take on twice as many school leavers. The State pays £750 for each split job, to help pay for the extra paper work. Details can be had from the Department of Employment, Freepost, London SW20 8TA.

Jobber See *Stockjobber*.

Jobber trade
Opening and closing the same number of *Futures contracts* for the same *Delivery month* on the same day.

Joint account
Although any two or more people can open a joint bank account, it is normally used by married people. But the husband and wife, or any other participants, must be clear what the account is for. Some couples use a joint account only to pay joint costs such as gas or electricity. Others pay

all their incomes into it and draw out as they please. This
requires a good mutual understanding. Joint accounts can
have legal advantages, particularly if one partner dies.

Jury service insurance
The Corporation of Lloyd's is a good place to turn to if you
fear the financial costs of being called for jury service. Jurors
are officially compensated, but at little more than the average
wage plus travelling and eating expenses. Well-paid and
self-employed people may suffer. A Lloyd's premium of,
say, £10 a year will buy you £20 a day for jury service for up
to 25 days.

Kaffirs
An old-fashioned term for South African gold-mining
shares.

Kerb trading
Dealing after the official *Close* of a market. The term stems
from the US habit of trading in the street after a market
shut, but the practice dates back to trading in London
outside the coffee houses before trading floors were
established.

Keynes, Lord
John Maynard Keynes (1883–1946) was a fellow of King's
College, Cambridge, who revolutionised *Classical economics*
with his *General Theory of Employment, Interest and Money*,
published in 1936. He produced a body of theory which
conferred a major economic role on the State's ability to
stimulate demand and confidence by public spending.
This introduced psychology as an important element in
economic management. Keynes also helped to set up the
International Monetary Fund in 1944.

Kina
The currency of Papua New Guinea, north of Australia. It
changes hands for about 75p.

Kip
The currency of communist-controlled Laos. The official
rate values the kip at about 2p, but there is a flourishing
black market whose rate appears to fluctuate wildly. For
tourists, the preferred foreign currencies are the US dollar
and the Thai baht.

Knock-for-knock
A way of short-circuiting motor insurance claims. In an
accident where there is shared or no blame, the insurers
each pay for repairs to the vehicles of their own policyholder,
rather than argue the toss. Motorists often feel they lose
by such bargains, but insurance firms argue that it keeps
down costs.

Kopek
The Russian rouble is worth 100 kopeks, a word formed in
1698 from 'kopyé', meaning 'lance'. In Latin script it is
sometimes spelt kopec, kopeck, kopeek, or copeck.

Koruna
The Czech currency. There are two rates: for commercial
deals a koruna is valued at about 9p, but tourists get
around 20 to the pound, making their korunas worth only
5p.

Krona
Sweden and Iceland call their currencies the krona, or
crown. The Swedish is worth 10p, the Icelandic 2p.

Krone
Like its cousin the krona, this is the Scandinavian for
'crown'. Denmark and its dependencies, the Faroe Islands
and Greenland, value their krone at around 7p. In Norway,
though, it is worth 10p.

Krugerrand
This is a South African coin containing precisely one ounce

of 24-carat gold. As such, it is a very convenient way for
small savers to invest in gold. Once the South African
authorities cottoned on to this, they introduced one-tenth,
one-quarter and half-sized versions. However, you do pay a
little more to cover the cost of minting the coin, and the
packaging of small amounts. A single coin can cost 20%
more than the free market bullion price, and a bank will
charge you more to buy it back. But if you think that gold
is going to rocket, krugerrands at least get you on the
launch pad. Krugerrands bought in the UK carry VAT.

Kwacha
An East African currency, common to both Malawi and
Zambia. They are each worth about 40p.

Kwanza
The currency of Angola, the former Portuguese colony in
central Africa. The kwanza is worth around 2p.

Kyat
The currency of Burma, pronounced 'chat'. Worth about
9p, it is divided into 100 pyas. Kyats are issued in 1-kyat
notes and coins, then in notes from five to 100 kyats. See
Pya.

Lading
To lade is an Old English word for 'load'. It survives in
common use as 'laden'. The shipping world uses it in the
phrase Bill of Lading, which asks payment for putting a
shipment on board.

Laissez faire
This French phrase became a slogan for free-market
economics from the seventeenth century onwards. It is an
abbreviation of 'laissez faire et laissez passer' – let things
happen and go on (without interference). See *Classical
economics*.

Land Registry

The government organisation which records the owners of
every slice of property in England and Wales. The head
office is at Lincoln's Inn Fields, London WC2, which can
put you in touch with district registries covering each
region. Scottish land is filed with the Sasine Register in
Edinburgh.

Last survivor policy

A type of *Life insurance* policy. It pays out only when the
last of a group of named people has died. It is commonly used
by husbands and wives, as it is cheaper than a policy on one
life, and can help to avoid *Inheritance Tax*.

Last trading day

The final day's trading in a particular *Delivery month*. Any
Futures contracts which have not been *Closed* by the end of
this day must be settled by *Delivery*, unless the two sides to
the contract agree otherwise.

Late retirement

In *Occupational pension* schemes, an employee can keep
working for an extra five years to build up his eventual
benefit, or a special increase can be awarded. The five-year
delay can also be applied to the *State pension*.

Law Society

The body which acts for all the solicitors in England and
Wales. If you do not know a firm of solicitors but need
legal advice, the Law Society can give you some names and
addresses. It also dispenses *Legal aid* and looks into
complaints against solicitors. If, however, your complaint
alleges that the solicitor has broken the law, you should
go to the police. The Law Society is at 113 Chancery Lane,
London WC2A 1PL. See also *Remuneration certificate*.

Lay-off

A worker is laid off if he or she is asked not to turn up for

work, but is kept on the payroll at a reduced wage.
Someone who is put on short-time working, to the extent
that his or her hours are cut by half or more, is also
regarded as laid off. The Employment Protection
(Consolidation) Act 1978 makes it compulsory for
companies to pay a minimum amount to employees laid off.
Check with your local Department of Employment office
for details. The address will be in the phone book. If the
lay-offs last for more than four weeks, or occur for *six*
weeks out of 13, the workers can claim *Statutory redundancy
payment*. However, the employer can fend this off by
promising that there will be normal work for at least 13
weeks. See *Redundancy*.

Leads and lags
This phrase is sometimes used to account for changes in a
country's *Balance of payments* or the value of its *Currency*
on foreign exchange markets. If a lot of importers lead, or
pay their bills early, this will swell the outflow of foreign
exchange. If they lag their payments it will have the opposite
effect, and conversely with exporters. If they think the
currency is going to fall, they will try to rush things, but if
they are confident of an appreciation they will slow
payments and receipts.

Lease
A lease is a contract whereby the owner of a property or
piece of equipment lets someone else have the use of it for an
agreed period, in return for a payment. Then it reverts to
the owner. 'Lease' can also mean the period of the lease
itself.

Leasing
This is a form of finance which has mushroomed in recent
years. If someone wants to use an expensive piece of
equipment, but either cannot afford to buy it or only needs
it for a short period, then it can be leased from someone
who does own it. In that sense, it is like renting or hiring.

But leasing has turned into big business because of the tax reliefs given to owners of equipment. This has attracted companies who have high profits and no easy ways of offsetting them – mainly the banks. They in turn are able to pass on part of their tax savings in relatively low leasing rates. And for many borrowing companies leasing has become a way of life because it does not affect their accounts as sharply as straightforward loans. The logic for the government condoning this merry-go-round is that it may encourage more new equipment to be produced, which helps to stimulate the economy.

Ledger
This is the book that lies – no, not in the sense of telling untruths (perish the thought), but in the literal meaning of the Saxon word, to lie, usually on a shelf by the window of a counting-house. The ledger records all the *Transactions* of a business, and is the basic tool of *Bookkeeping*. Nowadays, the stuff of ledgers has been transferred to computers. But the shelf it lay on is still called a ledge. See *Account*.

Legacy
A gift (though strictly speaking not of freehold property – see *Devise*) made through a *Will*. It is connected with the idea of delegating something to someone. As its origins are Latin, it is the word preferred by the legal profession, although it means the same as *Bequest*. There are several types of legacy: see *Demonstrative legacy*, *General legacy*, *Pecuniary legacy*, *Residuary legacy* and *Specific legacy*.

Legal aid
Legal aid is a grant from the government for people who cannot afford to go – or be taken – to law. The money is handed out by the *Law Society*. They can also tell you which solicitors will handle legal aid cases, as will *Citizens' Advice Bureaux*. How much aid you get depends on your savings, income and other financial details. The type of aid differs between civil, criminal and domestic cases. The latter come

under the *Green form* scheme. See also *Small Claims Court.*

Legal tender
Literally, legal tender is the amount and type of any coins
or notes you are allowed to tender in payment. It is not
illegal to accept more than the official limit. Bank of England
notes are legal tender in any amount, but Scottish ones only
in Scotland. Bronze coins are limited to 20p; cupro-nickel
(silver) 5p and 10p coins must not add up to more than
£5, and only £10 in silver 20p, 50p and £1 coins. There is
no limit on gold coins.

Lek
Albania's currency, valued at about 10p. Related, if only by
name, to the Bulgarian lev and Romanian leu.

Lempira
In the Honduras Republic, Central America, goods are
priced in terms of the lempira, which is worth about 40p.

Lender of last resort
In a financial crisis, everyone tries to pass the buck. When
the music stops, a business is liable to be caught in an
impossible position where it cannot meet its obligations.
That could provoke a series of collapses. So it is important
to have an agency which is willing to lend – at a price –
under any circumstances. That agency is normally the
Central Bank, which in turn has access to the government.
In Britain, the *Bank of England* is the lender of last resort.

Length of service
It is vital to know your exact length of service in a job when
it comes to calculating your *Notice period* – or *Statutory
redundancy payment.* Your local employment office can advise
you, but it is normally worked out in weeks, and any week
counts in which you worked at least 16 hours, or for which
you are covered by your *Contract of employment* – such as
illness. Strikes do not count, but neither do they break the

continuity of service. If your firm is taken over, or you
move to a different firm in the same group, there is no break.

Leone
The national currency of Sierra Leone, worth around 15p.

Letter of indemnity
If you lose a *Share certificate* you can get a replacement from
the company's registrar. But first you have to send a letter
of indemnity, in which you agree to bear any loss the
company suffers as a result of issuing the duplicate. It
often has to be countersigned by a bank.

Leu
The currency of Romania, where there is a commercial rate
of five to the pound but tourists get 15 for a pound. Its
name is related to the Albanian lek and Bulgarian lev.

Lev
Worth about 80p, the lev is Bulgaria's currency unit.
Related, if only by birth, to the Albanian lek and Romanian
leu.

Leverage See *Gearing*.

Liability
A financial liability is something you are liable to have to
pay back at some time. Most obvious is a loan, but people
forget that a company is also liable for shareholders' funds
and would have to pay them back in the event of a
break-up. These are both known as fixed liabilities. Current
liabilities include bank overdrafts, tax, dividend
payments, money owed to suppliers – and write-offs against
bad debts from customers.

Libra
Latin for pound, and the origin of the pound sterling, which
was at first literally a pound of sterling silver. It still survives
in today's £ sign. See *Pound, Solidus, Denarius*.

Licensed dealer
Under the Prevention of Fraud (Investments) Act 1958, all
professional dealers in *Securities* had to be licensed. But
one who was referred to simply as a licensed dealer was not
a member of the *Stock Exchange*, who were in any case
exempt.

Licensed deposit-taker
The secondary category of firm allowed to take deposits
from the public, under the *Banking Act 1979*. Licensed
deposit-takers have to be competently and prudently
managed, but do not have as high a standing as *Recognised
banks*. LDTs cannot call themselves banks without special
exemption from the *Bank of England*, which decides whether
a bank is a bank.

Lien
This comes from the Latin word *ligamen*, meaning a bond.
In English law a lien gives a creditor the right to hold on
to a debtor's property until the debt has been settled. That
is why legal documents sometimes speak of an asset being
acquired 'free of all liens and encumbrances'. An
encumbrance is another word for a lien or claim on a
property.

Life insurance
A sombre subject for many, because at stake is your life or
your spouse's. But it is a sensible way of insuring your
family against unexpected disaster, and there are a number
of variations on the theme to suit your own needs and
tastes. You bet the insurance firm that you will die by a
certain date – and, in the case of whole life insurance, that
you will die at some time. The insurer, like a bookmaker,
profits by adjusting the odds correctly. But also, because
of the time-scale, the insurer is able to invest your premiums
to the advantage of both sides. See *Term insurance,
Endowment insurance, Whole life insurance.*

LIFFE See *London International Financial Futures Exchange.*

Lilangeni
The currency of Swaziland, which lies between South Africa and Mozambique. The lilangeni is linked to the South African rand, at about three to the pound.

Limit order
This is an order given by an investor to a broker, setting limits at which to buy or sell a security. See *Day order, Fill or kill, Good till cancelled, Market order.*

Limited by guarantee
In most limited companies, the shareholders' liability is limited to the amount they have paid for their shares. But to make it easier to start certain businesses, particularly charities, the shareholders have only to promise that they will pay up if the company goes into *Liquidation.* In this way, their liability is limited by their guarantee, rather than by putting money in from the start. See *Limited company, Public limited company, Unlimited company, Partnership.*

Limited company
A legal entity which issues shares, the liability of shareholders being limited to the *Par value* of their shares. There are two main types of limited company in Britain: *Private companies* and *Public limited companies.* See also *Unlimited company, Limited by guarantee.*

Liquidator
Usually a trained accountant, a liquidator is appointed by creditors, shareholders or the Department of Trade to wind up a business by selling its assets, pay its debts and divide the remainder among the shareholders. See *Receiver.*

Lira
Rooted in the Roman word for a pound weight, libra, the lira is the currency of Italy and the associated territories

of San Marino and the Vatican. There are about 2,300 to
the pound. Turkey, which used to label its currency the
pound, has now adopted the name of the lira, with about
1,000 to the British pound.

Lloyd's, Corporation of
This is the world's biggest insurance market. Based in Lime
Street, in the east end of the City of London, it operates
in a similar way to the Stock Exchange. If you want to take
out a policy through Lloyd's, you go to a broker who is a
member there. When you have agreed what you want, he
goes into the market and asks the underwriters to make him
a quote. If he does not like the first quote, he can shop
around. In fact, the underwriters prefer to share the risks
among one another. It really caters for the big commercial
types of insurance, such as office blocks, supertankers and
jumbo jets, as well as the more highly-priced oddities like
concert pianist's hands. But Lloyd's prides itself on being
able to handle anything, so it does quite a bit of household
and motor insurance. The prices do tend to be keen, but
they tend to deal in standard packages.

Loan
If someone gives you something, especially money, on
condition that you return it, that is a loan. It usually has
to be returned within a specific time, and in the business
world there is always an *Interest* charge. Loans come in
many shapes and forms to meet the different needs of people
and companies. See *Borrowing, Personal loan, Bridging
loan, Overdraft, Advance, Collateral, Hire purchase,
Mortgage, Second mortgage, Debt, Loan capital, Debentures,
Credit cards* and *Credit union*.

Loan creditor
A technical term for someone who lends to a *Close company*
and so is regarded as a *Participator* in that company. It
does not include bankers, money brokers or stock jobbers
lending in the ordinary course of their business.

Loan Guarantee Scheme
A government plan to encourage banks to lend to small firms
which might otherwise be passed over. The government
can guarantee 70% of loans up to £75,000. In return the
banks pay the state a premium on the slice that has been
guaranteed.

Local authority bonds
Just as the government borrows money by issuing *Gilts*, so
local authorities do the same through bonds. These are
advertised in the press, and usually run for between one and
five years. The interest rate is often better than banks
offer. But they can be awkward to get rid of if you want to
cash in early. There is no open market in small sizes of
these bonds, and the local authorities themselves may
penalise you for cashing in early.

Local housing strategy
This is a plan submitted by local authorities to central
government, claiming what it sees as its housing needs for the
coming year in terms of new housing, improvement grants
and loans for home ownership or *Housing associations*.

London Commodity Exchange
This is the body which regulates the markets in the soft or
non-metal commodities like cocoa, coffee, grain, rubber,
sugar and wool. The LCE provides trading floors for these
markets, sets rules and settles disputes. There is an
individual association for each commodity. The LCE's
address is Cereal House, 58 Mark Lane, London EC3R
7NE.

London Enterprise Agency
This is a small-firm service set up by large firms – Barclays
Bank, British Petroleum, BOC International, GEC, IBM
(UK), ICFC, Marks and Spencer, Midland Bank and Shell
UK. It offers training and *Counselling*, and tries to put
small firms in touch with lenders or investors. The address

is 69 Cannon Street, London EC4N 5AB. See *Council for
Small Industries in Rural Areas, New Enterprise Programme,
Small Business Course, Small Firms Service, Business Expansion
Scheme.*

London International Financial Futures Exchange
This is a market based in the old Royal Exchange building,
near the Bank of England in the City of London. It deals in
contracts to deliver money, currency and other forms of
finance at fixed prices at a future date. Naturally the prices
of these contracts change from day to day, but once struck
they are fixed. This enables investors to insure against the
risk that the underlying price of, say, the US dollar might
go against them. The exchange opened on 30 September
1982.

London Metal Exchange
The City of London's centre for trading in the main metals
– aluminium, copper, lead, silver, tin and zinc. Founded in
1881, the trading floor is a ring spanning about 3.5 metres.
The merchants sitting round the ring trade from noon
until 1.10 p.m. During the break, 'official' prices are set,
and dealing resumes from 3.30 to 4.35 p.m. The exchange
is based at Plantation House, Fenchurch Street, London
EC3M 3AP.

Long
If you are long of a share, you own quite a lot of it or, in
other words, you have gone a *Bull* of it.

Loss adjuster
Someone employed by an insurance company to work out
the value of insured goods which have been lost or
damaged. Members of the Chartered Institute of Loss
Adjusters do not work for the public. The institute's
address is Mansfield House, 376 The Strand, London WC2R
0LR. See *Public loss assessor, Under-insurance.*

Lot
The size in which a Stock Exchange *market-maker* will deal at a given price, as displayed on the *SEAQ* screen.

Low start mortgage See *Endowment mortgage*,

Macro-economics
This deals with the problems of a total economy, and international relations between economies. It covers production, employment, price levels and the balance of payments. See *Micro-economics*.

Maintenance margin
The least a client must keep in his account with a broker on a *Futures* market, after deducting the amounts necessary for *Initial margin* and *Variation margin*. See also *Eligible margin*.

Maintenance payments
If you are paying or receiving maintenance you must check the tax position. Compulsory payments are tax deductible, voluntary are not. You may pay tax on what you receive, depending on how much you earn. Small payments direct to children are usually tax-free: best to have proof, like a bank account in their name. A solicitor will advise.

Man from the Pru See *Prudential Assurance* and *Home service insurance*.

Manpower Services Commission
Formed by the Employment and Training Act 1973, the MSC began life on 1 January 1974 to run the public employment and training services. It is accountable to the Department of Employment, but operates independently. It has two main operations dealing with the public: the *Employment Services Division* and *Training Services Division*. The head office is at Moorfoot, Sheffield, S1 4PQ. There are separate MSCs for Scotland and Wales. See also *Disabled*, *Project Fullemploy*, *Professional and Executive Recruitment*.

Manufacture
When it was first coined from the Latin in 1567, manufacture
referred only to making things by hand. But as *Industry*
became mechanised, manufacture inevitably was extended
to cover everything made in factories or workshops, in contrast
to agricultural products.

Manufacturing account
Because a manufacturer does not just buy and sell goods,
his accounts are more complicated than those of a retailer or
most other service firms. Raw materials go through various
stages of treatment to turn them into finished goods. This
involves *Work in progress*, and involves a clearer distinction
between *Direct expense* and *Overheads*.

Margin call
A demand for an investor on a *Futures* market to put up
more money because his *Futures contract* has gone against him.
See *Eligible margin, Variation margin*.

Mark
On the foreign exchanges the mark, or Deutschmark, is the
currency of West Germany. On the stock market a mark
is the price at which a stock or share bargain is struck. The
Stock Exchange publishes a figure for the daily number
of marks. While this gives some idea of how busy trading
was, it can be misleading. One mark can cover several
deals, and in any case jobbers are shy of giving too much
information about heavily traded shares as they do not
wish to give their own position away.

Market
A word beloved of economists and street salesmen alike. It
is a gathering of people to buy and sell similar things. Thanks
to modern telecommunications, the traders can be thousands
of miles away from one another. The test is whether 'the
prices obtainable in one part of the market affect the prices
paid in other parts', according to the philosopher Jeremy

Bentham. Economists base many of their theories on an
ideal called the perfect market, which dreams that
everyone in it knows instantly about everything there is to
know about the market. Happily, it does not exist in
reality.

Market capitalisation
The value that the stock market puts on a company's equity.
It is calculated by multiplying the share price by the
number of shares in issue.

Market if touched
A price order on a *Futures* market, that automatically
becomes a *Futures order* if the price is reached.

Market maker
A Stock Exchange firm which offers to quote a buying and
selling price in stocks or shares. Gilt-edged market makers
must be approved by the Bank of England. If firms want to
make markets in both gilts and equities, they must do so
separately. See also *Broker dealer, Inter dealer broker*.

Market order
A *Futures* market order for a broker to buy or sell at the best
price he can get. See *At best, Day order, Fill or kill, Good till
cancelled, Limit order, Market if touched*.

Markka
The currency unit of Finland, valued at around 12p.

Mark-up See *Profit margin*.

Marriage
An important event financially. The government, keen to
encourage happy families, gives tax concessions to married
couples. If both partners are working, the combined income
can also help to get a bigger mortgage – although building
societies are more flexible than they were about couples who

live together without marrying. See *Married man's allowance*, *Separate assessment*, *Separate taxation*, *Child benefit*.

Married man's allowance
When a couple get married, the husband's *Personal allowance* is upgraded from the *Single person's* to the *Married man's* – usually about 50% more. In the year of the marriage, he gets a proportion of the allowance, depending on which month the great event occurs in. If you marry in April, he gets the whole lot but an October wedding ranks for half the rate.

Married Women's Property Acts
Passed in 1870 and 1882, these Acts have a bearing on *Life insurance* policies. A husband can take out a policy on his own life, with the proviso that the proceeds go straight into a *Trust* and do not form part of his *Estate*. The wife can do the same thing in the opposite direction.

Matching
At the end of a day's trading on a financial or commodity market, the deals have to be checked to make sure that in each case the buyer and seller agree about the number and price of what they have traded.

Maternity benefit
The State pays two types of benefit to see a mother through the financial strain of birth. A weekly allowance is paid for the weeks surrounding the birth, the amount depending on *National Insurance* contributions. There is also a *Maternity grant* to help pay for clothing, cot, buggy and rattle.

Maternity grant
Every mother can claim a maternity grant. You must get form BM4 from your local clinic or social security office. The scheme is explained fully in leaflet NI.17A. See *Maternity benefit*.

Maternity leave
If a woman has been working in the same place for two
years, she can claim maternity leave, entitling her to stop
work for 29 weeks and return to the same job without
breaking her *Length of service*. If there is no job to come back
to, she is regarded as having been dismissed on the day she
planned to return. Redundancy payments will be based
on service up to that date.

Maturity
The period when a *Futures contract* can be settled by *Delivery*.
It begins with the *First notice day* and ends with the *Last
trading day* of the contract. When a *Financial instrument* or
a security reaches maturity, that is the time for the
investors to get their money back.

Maximum price fluctuation
The biggest amount the price of a *Futures contract* can change
during one trading session. It is fixed by the authorities
running the particular market. Once the price reaches the
limit, trading in that contract is halted for a time, to
allow everyone to cool off. Then trading restarts
without limit.

Means test
A test applied by a local authority or central government
department to decide whether someone is entitled to
financial help. It is a test of the person's means, in terms of
how much they earn and have saved. While this seems all very
reasonable, means tests became an emotional issue in the
1930s, largely because they were carried out on the basis
of the whole household, as opposed to the individuals within
it. This cut across the financial customs and habits within
each family, and could prove highly embarrassing if, for
example, an aged relative had squirrelled away a large sum
which might debar the whole family from State help. That
system was scrapped in 1948.

Medical accidents See *Action for the Victims of Medical Accidents*.

Medical insurance
If you are ill, and do not want to go to a National Health Service hospital, you have two possible financial problems: how to pay for a private bed, and how to make up income lost through being off work. The first can be solved with an insurance policy through British United Provident Association or Private Patients Plan. Your premiums will depend on the fees at the hospital you want to go to, and how much you will be able to meet the bills yourself. Loss of income can be covered through Permanent Health Insurance, which gives you an agreed weekly sum if you can no longer work – something which is more likely than accidental death. Premiums here can be trimmed by accepting a delay between your loss of job and the onset of payments.

Memorandum of association
When every company is formed, it must lodge at *Companies House*, a part of the Department of Trade and Industry, a memorandum of association. This states the company's intended activities – property developer, widget maker – and outlines its objects and structures. See *Articles of association*.

Mercantilism
Based on the mercantile, or *Merchant*, view of politics, mercantilism was elevated into a major crusade in the sixteenth and seventeenth centuries. The idea was that the strength of the nation revolved round monetary wealth, and that therefore everything should be done to help exporters by protecting home industries and curbing movements of *Gold*.

Merchant
A merchant is someone who buys and sells goods on a *Wholesale* basis for a *Profit*. It was originally bound up

with the Latin and French for 'market', but it has long since
been broadened beyond that. The word is also used as an
adjective, as in the Merchant Navy and *Merchant banks*. The
adjective for someone who has a merchant-like approach
to business is mercantile, which overlaps confusingly with
Mercantilism: see separate entry.

Merchant bank
This is a particular type of bank in the City of London. It
does not deal with the public, and does not issue *Cheques*
or take *Deposits*. Instead, merchant banks grew to finance
the trade of merchants. This requires special skills. The
banker has to have some knowledge of the trade in question,
whether the two sides to a contract will fulfil their sides of
the bargain, and how feasible the deal is in the first place.
The modern merchant bank does much more than that, going
into all sorts of *Corporate finance*, including share *Flotations*
and *Takeovers*. The top merchant banks belong to the
Accepting Houses Committee.

Merger
A merger is the union of two companies. It is often used as
a polite word to describe what is really the takeover of one
company by another. But a merger implies a roughly equal
partnership. As a rule of thumb, the bigger of the two
should not have more than three times the assets of the
smaller. And watch to see how the boardroom seats are
divided up after the deal.

Metical
The currency of Mozambique in East Africa. Changes hands
at about 2p.

Micro-economics
This is the part of economics that deals with individuals,
industries and companies, as opposed to *Macro-economics*.

Middle price
In most of the financial markets, two prices are quoted for

each security. One is the buying price and the other is the selling. As a form of shorthand, people outside the market quote a price halfway between, to give an idea of how it has moved during the day. This middle price is the one used by newspapers for share prices, although the *Financial Times* quotes the double price for currencies and some other items. See *Spread*.

Mini-budget
A phrase which came into vogue in the 1970s, when Denis Healey as Chancellor of the Exchequer took to making *Budget* proposals several times a year, instead of confining himself to the big day in March or April. The thinking behind this was to be more flexible, and get away from the idea of Budget Day as the make-or-break, once-for-all chance to get the economy right. But he was derided for his efforts as a tinkerer and publicity-monger. That's politics.

Minimum price fluctuation See *Basis point, Maximum price fluctuation*.

MIRAS See *Mortgage Investment Relief At Source*.

Misrepresentation Act
An attempt to reinforce the *Sale of Goods Act*'s provisions regarding accurate description of goods. You can claim misrepresentation if the seller lies to persuade you to buy, and the lie actually helped to persuade you. It does not apply to opinions like 'best value anywhere', and can be difficult to prove unless you get the salesman to write his claims. However, unlike the *Trade Descriptions Act*, this one does cover property deals and sales by private individuals.

MIT See *Market if touched*.

Mobility allowance
If you are over 5 years old and under 65, and are unable to get about on your own, you may be able to claim mobility

allowance to help you pay for equipment to solve the
problem. It is a weekly sum which should be regularly
increased to make up for the effects of inflation. See
Disability benefit.

Monetarism
An economic theory which tries to explain the cause of
inflation. As expounded by Professor Milton Friedman,
monetarism blames governments for printing money faster
than the economy is growing. Result: more money than
goods, forcing prices up. This was a cornerstone of the 1979
Conservative government's economic policy, which aimed
at reducing inflation by cutting its own borrowing.
Opponents argue that it would be better to stimulate
production so that it catches up with the growth of money.
See *Economics, Friedman, Keynes, Quantity theory of money.*

Monetary working capital
Accountants' jargon for the money needed to run a business
from day to day. It includes bills owing and owed, the
up-to-date value of stocks and the daily ins and outs of the
firm's bank account. See *Current cost accounting.*

Money
Money is anything which everyone in an economy will accept
as payment for goods and services. It should be easy to carry,
and is much fairer if it is not something people want to
consume. In 1945 cigarettes were used as money in
Germany – which was good news for non-smokers. You do
not even need the bits of paper and metal we use: in the
cashless society money could just be an electronic
scoreboard, changing the entries in our bank accounts. Money
is a way of pricing things, and telling you how much you
have saved . . . or how much you owe.

Money at call See *Call.*

Money broker
There are two forms of money broker in the City. The more

widely known deals for banks, corporations and other big
clients to place spare cash or make up shortages, taking a
commission on the way. The Stock Exchange has its own
version, whose job is to enable *market makers* to borrow
either stock or money from institutions so that they can meet
their commitments at the end of each *Account*.

Moneylender
A last resort for anyone who needs to borrow money but has
been turned down by everyone else. They tend to lend only a
few hundred pounds. For most of their customers that is
enough. But the interest rate will be high. If you have to
go to a moneylender, try to make sure he or she is licensed.
Then at least you will have some comeback if things go
wrong. See also *Pawnbroker*.

Money market
Less specialised than the *Discount market*, the City's money
market deals in all forms of short-term *Loans* between
companies, banks and local authorities. It is, in effect, a
buffer for spare cash and temporary cash shortages. Unlike
the *Discount market*, it does not deal directly with the Bank
of England, but the money brokers take their cue from
signals sent from the Bank – as does everyone in the City.
While discount houses tend to make loans themselves,
money brokers prefer simply to take a fee for putting
borrower and lender together. It is less risky, but it does
put them at the mercy of a downturn in the level of business.

Money shop
A friendlier phrase for a bank aimed at the man in the street.
It will take and pay out cash, and offer a limited range of
personal services such as insurance. See also *Share shop*.

Money stocks
A stock market term for *Gilts* which have a very short life,
so that they are themselves very close to being money.

Money supply

Money is supplied to an economy in various forms. The most obvious is notes and coins, but a bank loan is another way of supplying money. It can also come from abroad, in the form of payments for exports. Economists use different definitions of money, according to what they are trying to analyse. The most basic is called M1 and includes notes, coins and sterling bank deposits. The other major version is called M3. This is M1 plus deposits with *Discount houses*, *Merchant banks* and foreign banks in the UK. It is directly affected by changes in the *Public Sector Borrowing Requirement*. See also *Domestic credit expansion*, *Monetarism*.

Monopolies and Mergers Commission

Created in its original form in 1948, the Monopolies and Mergers Commission is a statutory body which is asked by the Secretary of State for Trade to investigate mergers which may produce a monopoly, or monopoly problems already existing in a certain industry. It can examine any merger which brings together at least £15m of assets, or would give the combined group more than 25% of a market. The Trade Secretary can accept recommendations to prevent such a merger, but in practice he can do little to unwind an existing monopoly. See *Office of Fair Trading*.

Monopoly

A monopoly is an economist's nightmare, where there is only one seller of a product. In theory this gives the monopolist great power to decide the price and supply of that product, depending on how much demand there is for it. In practice, there are few products which people will pay any price for, or where it is impossible to produce a near-substitute. Governments occasionally create monopolies, such as postal services, telephones or railways. Prices have tended to be higher in those cases. See also *Monopsony* and *Monopolies and Mergers Commission*.

Monopsony
A monopsony is a buyer's monopoly, so that there is only
one buyer of a product in a particular market. This can make
life difficult for the producers. There are several cases of
very big industrial buyers who give their suppliers the
run-around, but true monopsonists are usually governments
who put themselves in that position by law. Military
equipment is an example.

Mortgage
The passport to the property-owning society. Britain is
divided into those who rent their home and those who buy
– which inevitably means having a mortgage. The buyers
are now in the majority, as young couples raced to jump
aboard the bandwagon to what seemed to be a near-certain
paper profit, all helped by generous tax allowances. In the
mid-1970s, however, many found that the profits were by
no means assured, and successive Chancellors of the
Exchequer took some of the fun out of the game by not
increasing the £25,000 mortgage ceiling on tax relief, until
moves were made to raise it to £30,000 in 1983. The
mortgage itself is like hire purchase on a grand scale,
involving monthly repayments over periods of up to 35
years. It can also be used to extend your house – or to buy
a boat.

Mortgage Investment Relief At Source (MIRAS)
A scheme to simplify tax relief on mortgage interest.
Previously, borrowers paid the full interest to the banks
or building societies and received the relief through a change
in their *Tax code*. Now lenders deduct *Basic rate* tax from
the interest element in the monthly payment. Higher-rate
taxpayers get the extra back through the Inland Revenue.
Lenders of £30,000+ mortgages can opt not to operate
MIRAS.

Mortgage protection policy
This is a life insurance policy taken out to ensure that the

balance of a house *Mortgage* will be paid if the family breadwinner dies. It is the cheapest form of cover for a mortgage. See *Endowment mortgage*.

Motor insurance
The Road Traffic Act 1972 demands that you at least insure yourself against the cost of injuring someone else on the public highway. Some drivers are such bad risks that this is all the cover they can get, but for the rest of us there are three more grades of motor insurance. Third Party adds cover against damaging other people's cars or property. Third Party, Fire and Theft also pays if your car is stolen or burnt. Comprehensive extends the insurance to repairs to your car after an accident. Your premium will vary with the type of cover, your age, sex, job, record, address, make of car and the ever-growing cost of repairs. See *Claim*, *Cover*, *Excess*, *Knock-for-knock*, *No-claims bonus*, *Travel insurance*.

Multiple agency
This is an agreement whereby you ask several estate agents to try to sell your house. It gives you more chances, but each agent may ask a higher percentage commission to make up for the fact that his chances are lower. They are unlikely to push your house so hard, either. See *Estate agent*, *Sole agency*, *Sole selling rights*.

Mutual Aid Centre
A charity devoted to setting up self-help workshops for consumer goods repairs as well as local pressure groups such as commuter clubs. Its address is 18 Victoria Park Square, London E2 9PF. See also *National Federation of Consumer Groups*.

Mutual fund
This is the name for the American equivalent of British *Unit Trusts*. They do not operate on exactly the same basis – after all, they stem from quite different legal systems – but both invest in stocks and shares on behalf of their customers.

Mutual insurance companies

Many *Insurance* companies operate like any other limited
liability companies in other industries. Their capital is put
up by shareholders, who collect dividends out of profits.
But in Britain several of the major insurance firms are
mutual. That is to say, if you take out a policy with one of
them, you automatically become a part-owner of the
company and all the money in the life fund is there for the
benefit of policyholders. That sounds like a better deal for
policyholders, but in practice there is very little to choose
between the performance of the big firms of either type.
However, you may feel more comfortable with one than
another. Mutual insurance companies are nothing to do with
Mutual funds.

Naira

Nigeria's currency unit, valued at 60p.

Naked writer

A daring type of investor. He is willing to write, to sell, an
option on a share in the *Traded option* market, without owning
any of the shares himself. He is gambling that the share
price will go down sufficiently to make the option
worthless, at which point he will not be asked to deliver the
shares. But if a naked writer is wrong, he can lose a lot
more than his pin-striped suit.

National Association of Conveyancers

This organisation represents conveyancing firms. These are
specialists in *Conveyancing* who claim to charge less than
solicitors. However, the legal establishment is inevitably
making life difficult for them to break the traditional
monopoly – worth millions a year to solicitors – in legal fees
for moving house. Worth considering if the house deal
looks straightforward. The association's address is 2
Chichester Rents, London, WC2 1EG. They can put you
in touch with one of their members.

National Association of Securities Dealers and Investment Managers

This is a revamped version of the Association of Licensed Dealers in Securities, which was founded in 1979. It has about 1,000 members and aims to improve standards in the business, develop its members' contribution to UK securities markets, and represent its members' interests to the government. See *Licensed dealer*.

National Children's Bureau

A body representing leading children's charities. It acts as a link between the charities and the government, banks and potential donors. It operates a special bond under which people can get tax relief on loans without having to commit themselves to a *Covenant*. The money is divided among the member charities. The bureau's address is 8 Wakley Street, London EC1V 7QE.

National Consumer Council

Publishes reports on consumer topics, and lobbies on behalf of the consumers at government level. Not totally independent, as it is sponsored by the government, which set the council up in 1975. It does not handle individual complaints. See *Consumer law*, *National Federation of Consumer Groups*.

National Council for Industrial Language Training See *Industrial Language Training Service*.

National Economic Development Council

An attempt to achieve economic growth by edict. Set up in 1962, its job was 'coordinating all the major expansion plans of British industry' by finding ways of increasing the rate of growth and considering obstacles to growth. It has a full-time staff, but the council itself includes the main economics ministers, led by the Chancellor of the Exchequer, as well as representatives of industrial management and the trades unions. There are a series of 'little Neddies' covering individual industries. The address is 21 Millbank, London SW1P 4QX.

National Enterprise Board See *British Technology Group*.

National Institute for Economic and Social Research
An independent, non-profit-making body, better known for its economic than its social research. It produces a quarterly report containing forecasts for the UK economy. Founded in 1938, the institute has a reputation for putting forward strong alternatives to the UK Treasury's official view of the economy. It is based at 2 Dean Trench Street, London SW1P 3HE.

National Insurance
National Insurance, created in 1911 by David Lloyd George, is the basis of Britain's social security system. It is modelled on private insurance and pension schemes, in that the public pay regular contributions which are invested and used to finance unemployment benefit, sickness benefit and the *State pension*. However, successive governments have failed to keep the money in a water-tight compartment, and it is now regarded as another source of revenue alongside taxes. It is, in effect, a payroll tax. The rates of the various benefits are, inevitably, determined by the politicians rather than the actuaries.

National Research and Development Corporation See *British Technology Group*.

National Savings
The National Savings Department is a government body which stems from a savings drive during the first world war. It operates through the Post Office, and by post. There are *National Savings Bank Ordinary and Investment Accounts*, *National Savings Certificates*, *Premium Bonds*, *Index-Linked Certificates* and *Save As You Earn*.

National Savings Bank Ordinary Account
This is a savings account through the Post Office. The
interest rate is low, though some of it is tax-free. But it can
suit some people better than a *Current account* with a bank,
for you can withdraw £100 on demand. See *National Savings,*
National Savings Investment Account.

National Savings Certificates
These are certificates issued through the Post Office by the
National Savings Department. They are tax-free, which is
good for high taxpayers. The standard type pays interest on
a rising scale for up to five years, although you get nothing
if you cash in during the first year. In recent years, the high
rate of inflation has put the spotlight on two other forms of
National Savings: *Index-Linked Certificates* and *Save As You*
Earn. See also *Premium Bonds*.

National Savings Investment Account
This is the longer-term counterpart of the *National Savings*
Ordinary Account. You have to give a month's notice of
withdrawals, but the interest rate tends to be as good as in
a building society and is paid before tax deductions. That
does not mean it is tax-free, but it is handier for
non-taxpayers.

National wealth
Like *Wealth* itself, this is a phrase with many meanings.
Economists use it to refer to the monetary value of all the
property and all the buildings and all the businesses in the
country: a pretty meaningless figure which is used to make
comparisons with similarly meaningless figures from other
countries. How much would a Chinaman pay for an
English black pudding factory? Would a Texan outbid an
Indian for a sacred cow? Some argue that the best wealth is
the sort that is impossible to value, like the Lake District
or the Scottish Highlands.

Nearby futures
The nearest active trading month of a *Futures* market – as
opposed to *Deferred ftures*.

NEDC See *National Economic Development Council*.

NEDO
The National Economic Development Office, which serves
the *National Economic Development Council*.

Net
Based on the old French word for 'neat', net came to mean
a sum of money which was not liable to any deductions,
or that all deductions had already been made from the *Gross*
amount. A typical use is in analysing company *Profits*, when
the gross trading profit is whittled down to a net profit after
deducting items like interest charges and tax.

Net assets per share
The book value of assets in a company, divided by the
number of shares issued by that company. 'Book value'
refers to the value put on the assets in the *Balance sheet*. The
real value, especially of any property, may be higher and other
assets may be worth less than book value. But it is the only
clear yardstick to take. Certain assets are excluded
altogether from this calculation – mainly intangibles such as
Goodwill.

Net Asset Value
This is one of the ways of judging the value of a share. The
Shareholders funds in a company's *Balance sheet*, less any
intangible assets like *Goodwill*, are divided by the number
of shares issued. This gives a net asset value per share,
which can be compared with the price of the shares on the
stock market. If the NAV is higher than the share price,
then the shares have a solid backing, but it may be that the
management is not making the most of the assets. If the
share price is higher than the NAV, the company is probably

quite highly rated but may be vulnerable to any mishap.
In theory, the NAV is what shareholders should collect if
the company were to be broken up, but in practice it gives
little guide as many of the assets would fetch a lower price
than their book value.

Net position
The number of *Futures contracts* bought or sold which have
not been offset by deals in the opposite direction on a
Futures market.

Net profit
After a firm's *Trading account* has been worked out, the next
accountancy step is to knock off items like directors' pay,
depreciation, tax and the accountant's own fees, to arrive at
the net profit. This shows how much is left to be
transferred to the firm's *Capital account* or *Reserves*. In
Limited companies it is often called the net attributable
profit, struck after dividends have been paid. See
Bookkeeping, Final account.

Net replacement cost
This is the current value of an asset in a business. It is
worked out by discovering the *Gross replacement cost* of the
asset, and making a deduction to allow for how old it is. See
Replacement cost.

Net worth (of a company) See *Net asset value*.

New Enterprise Programme
A TOPS course run by the *Training Services Division* of the
Manpower Services Commission, for people who want to start
businesses which the MSC considers have 'real potential for
growth'. Less ambitious folk can be put on a *Small business
course*, also run by the MSC, whose head office is at
Moorfoot, Sheffield, S1 4PQ. See also *Small Firms Service,
CoSIRA, London Enterprise Agency, Business Expansion
Scheme*.

New-for-old insurance
At one time, *Household insurance* policies were cast on the basis that payment on a claim would be enough to pay for a lost or damaged item only after wear-and-tear. Inflation made a nonsense of that, so now insurers are urging us to pay more in return for policies which will buy brand-new replacements.

Ngultrum
The currency of Bhutan, worth 18 to the pound. See *Rupee*.

NIESR See *National Institute for Economic and Social Research*.

No-claims bonus
A device for cutting the number of claims on motor policies. The insurer gives drivers a discount on their premiums if they have not claimed on the policy in the past year. The discount can be 60%. While this may give the driver a nice warm feeling, the effect is to deter him from making a claim, for fear of losing some or all of that bonus. This can make it worth the policyholder's while to pay repair bills of up to £200 or so out of his own pocket. See *Motor insurance*.

Nominal account
As part of the process of calculating the profit and loss of a business, nominal accounts are kept which show profits or losses on different activities. They are called nominal because the money is there in name only: their purpose is to show how the business is doing. On the loss side, they can include wages, salaries, postage and rent. Profits can include rent received, commission received or professional fees received.

Nominal capital See *Authorised capital*.

Nominal income
Wages and salaries expressed in cash terms, without making

any allowance for the effects of inflation or deflation. See *Real income*.

Non-pensionable earnings

This is a tax term for the pay of those who are not part of an *Occupational pension* scheme – mainly company directors and the self-employed. Instead they can put part of their earnings into a retirement annuity scheme approved by the Inland Revenue, who will then give *Tax* relief on these contributions.

Non-profit-making organisation

This is the general term for voluntary organisations whose main aim is not to make a profit. It may be a sports club, a charity, a political association or an amateur dramatics society. Although it is not the object to make a profit, such clubs must still pay their way and have proper *Accounts* and *Bookkeeping*. See *Accumulated fund*.

Non-resident

In tax terms, a non-resident can escape UK tax. But to qualify, they have to live outside Britain for a minimum period each year, currently about six months. See *Tax haven*.

Normal retirement age

The *State pension* age is fixed, currently at 65 for men and 60 for women. But in *Occupational pension schemes* the 'normal' age can be between 60 and 70 for men and 55 and 70 for women, with some flexibility for special cases such as risky or strenuous jobs. The *Occupational Pensions Board* can advise. In *Self-employed pensions* the age limits are 60 to 75. See *Early retirement, Late retirement*.

Notice of coding

Whenever the Inspector of Taxes changes your *Tax code*, he sends you a notice of coding. This sets out your allowances, and from the total deducts any offsets such as untaxed interest. See *P45, P60, Pay As You Earn, Tax deduction card*.

Notice period
When you start a new job, in most cases you should be given
a *Contract of employment* which clearly states your notice
period. This is the amount of notice you or your boss must
give one another if either of you decides to end your job.
If you do not think the period is long enough, go to the local
Citizens' Advice Bureau or legal aid centre to check your
rights. If you are working full time your notice period should
be at least a week.

NRDC See *British Technology Group*.

Numbered bank account
A speciality of Switzerland, but also offered by other
countries. The point is that these accounts are known only by
a number, not a name, and only the bank and the account
holder know who the account holder is. The Swiss
authorities have loosened the secrecy a little, however, where
crime is suspected.

Occupational pension
This is a pension provided by an employer, and you both
pay in. It is tied to your occupation. If you leave the firm
after five years but before pension age, your contributions
can be frozen until retirement. Most schemes nowadays
are based on a fraction of your salary on the day you retire.
Your pension in such schemes will be 1/60th or 1/80th of
that salary for every year you have worked for the firm.
After 20 years you would get 20/60ths – a third – or 20/
80ths, equal to a quarter. You can usually take some of your
entitlement in a lump sum, and there should be provision
for widows. See *Occupational Pensions Board, Pension, State
pension, Supernanuation Funds Office, Additional Voluntary
Contribution, Company Pensions Information Centre, Early
retirement, Late retirement, Normal retirement age.*

Occupational Pensions Board
This is a body set up under the Social Security Pensions Act

1975 to supervise *Occupational pensions*. Companies are
entitled to *Contract out* of the *State pension's additional
component*, and provide employees with a private scheme. The
OPB's job is to ensure that these schemes stay up to scratch.
It works hand-in-hand with the Inland Revenue's
Superannuation Funds Office, which is concerned with the
tax aspect. They are both at Apex Tower, High Street,
New Malden, Surrey. See also *Company Pensions Information
Centre*.

OECD See *Organisation for Economic Co-operation and
Development*.

Offer
The offer price of a stock market *Share* or a *Unit trust* is the
price at which the security is on offer to you – the selling
price. It is always higher than the price for buying back
from you, known as the *Bid* price. An offer is also a
newspaper shorthand for a *Takeover* bid.

Offer for sale
This is a method of floating a company's shares on the stock
exchange. A prospectus is published, giving details about the
company. So many shares are then offered for sale to the
public at a fixed price or by tender. Once the shares have
been posted to the investors who applied for them, dealings
begin on the market, which may well not agree that the
fixed price is the right one. See also *Tender* and *Introduction*.

Office of Fair Trading
A body set up by the Department of Trade to act as a
watchdog for cases of unfair trading. It looks at all mergers
involving combined assets of over £15m, to see if the
Secretary of State for Trade should refer the deal to the
Monopolies and Mergers Commission. The OFT also carries
out its own investigations into such topics as secondhand car
sales and plumbing, and either produces publicity to make
the public more aware or suggests changes in the law.

Official Receiver
Under the Bankruptcy Acts, the Department of Trade
appoints an official *Receiver* to manage the property of a
bankrupt person until a trustee is appointed. They also wind
up companies when there is no creditors' or shareholders'
money to pay for a *Liquidator*. See *Receiving order*.

Offshore funds
To escape UK tax, investment funds have been set up in
friendly territories with gentler tax laws. As the UK is a group
of islands, any funds based outside them are known as
offshore. Thanks to historical hiccups, the most popular
are part of the UK but have clung to special status, like the
Channel Islands and the Isle of Man. You can find these
funds advertised in the newspapers. Most, however,
stipulate a high minimum investment before they will take
your money. See *Tax haven*.

Oligopoly
The *Monopoly* of the few, where a few sellers dominate a
market and the action of any one of them influences the
others. In real life, it can be all too tempting for the
oligopolists to get together and arrange things between
them. See *Cartel* and *Restrictive Practices Court*.

One-parent families
If you find yourself having to bring up your family alone,
check as soon as possible with your local *Social Security* office,
Citizens' Advice Bureau or *Legal Aid Centre* on your rights.
You can certainly claim an extra tax allowance. Extra may
be available for those with large families or low incomes.

Open a position See *Position*.

Open contract
On a *Futures* market, an open contract is one which has been
bought or sold without any offsetting deal to close it by a
sale or purchase respectively, or by taking *Delivery* of the
underlying *Financial instrument* or *Commodity*.

Open interest
The total number of *Open contracts* which have been bought
on a *Futures* market, and have not yet been closed.

Open market operations
Although governments can do much to operate the economic
levers through *Budgets* and other changes in the law, the most
effective way to influence interest rates, the amount of credit
and even the level of confidence is by intervening directly in
the money and stock markets through the *Bank of England*.
The Bank can inject cash by buying *Gilts*, or squeeze the
system by selling them. It can also smooth the ups and
downs of the *Discount market*. Above all, members of these
markets always watch closely to see what the Bank is up to.

Open order
An order on a financial market that stands until it has been
executed by the broker, or cancelled.

Open outcry
On most markets, dealing is done quietly and discreetly
between the buyer and seller or their representatives such
as *Stockbrokers*. But on *Futures* markets, the open outcry
system is used, in which the dealers stand on the floor of
the exchange, sometimes called the *Pit*, and shout their bids
for contracts, or offers of contracts. The effect is that
everyone knows what is going on, but it is a system which
works well only when there is plenty of action.

Opportunity cost
Most people think that when they buy something, all it costs
them is money. Economists have produced the more
interesting notion that what it really costs is the opportunity
to buy something else. Economics is about choice: a bigger
house or a new car, a packet of cigarettes or a pint of beer.
The delusion is to think that we can have both, for in that
case there is always a third choice which has to be given up.

Option

The right to buy an asset at a preset price over an agreed span of time. How much you pay for the option depends what you think is going to happen to the value of the asset over the option period. See *Traded options*.

Option mortgages

These are designed for home-buyers who pay little or no *Income tax*. The rate of interest is subsidised by the government, but there is no tax relief on the interest. It is a way of spreading the home-ownership habit, but it is still harder in the early years because most of the mortgage repayment is repaying capital rather than interest. A more serious problem is that the borrower may do well enough in his career to pay full tax rates, giving him the worst of both worlds. There is a switching facility, but you have to be careful with the timing.

Order of liquidity

When a *Bookkeeper* is preparing a *Balance sheet*, he can lay out the assets and liabilities in one of two ways: the order of liquidity and the *Order of permanence*. The order of liquidity starts with the most liquid assets and works down to the most permanent. Depending on the type of business, the order of assets could be cash in hand, cash at bank, debtors, stock, motor vehicles, furniture, plant and machinery, land and buildings. Banks prefer this method. The order of permanence works the other way round.

Order of permanence

This is one way a *Bookkeeper* can lay out the items in a *Balance sheet*. On the assets side, he would start with the fixed assets – land and buildings, plant and machinery, furniture and motor vehicles. Then he would go on to the current assets – stock, debtors, cash at bank and cash in hand. The other approach is the *Order of liquidity*, which starts from the opposite direction. The order of permanence

is favoured by manufacturers, because of the importance
of the factory to their business.

Ordinary dividend
A *Dividend* paid on ordinary *Shares*.

Ordinary share See *Share*.

Ordinary share account
This is a building society savings account. It is as safe as a
bank and usually pays a little more to *Basic rate* taxpayers.
The share element stems from the structure of building
societies, which gives every holder of a share account a vote
at annual meetings. Most societies will let you have £500 on
demand from these accounts, and more at a few days'
notice. See *Building society*, *Subscription share account*, *Term
share*, *Escalator share*.

**Organisation for Economic Co-operation and
Development**
Originally set up to organise Europe's economic recovery
after 1945, it is now largely a discussion and study group.
Based in Paris, the OECD has 24 nation-members. They
include all the main western European countries, together
with the US, Canada and Japan.

Original document
The raw data of *Bookkeeping*, original documents are the
hard evidence of each *Transaction* in a business. They can
be receipts, invoices, hire purchase contracts or complex
legal documents. See also *Day book*.

OTC See *Over-the-counter market*.

Ouguiya
The currency of Mauritania, the West African state just
south of Morocco. The ouguiya is worth about 1p.

Output
Output is what is put out, or produced, by an economic unit

– an individual worker, a company, an industry, an economy or the whole world.

Output tax See *Value-Added Tax*.

Overcall See *Angel*.

Overcapitalised
This refers to the rare case when a company has more *Capital* than it needs for the level of business it is doing. *Turnover* may shrink, of course, in bad times, but even then companies find they have to pay for their premises. See *Overtrading*, *Undercapitalised*.

Overdraft
An overdraft is the type of loan you can award yourself – but your bank manager will not be amused. Whenever you draw out of your account more than there is in it, you have got an overdraft. Bankers naturally prefer this to happen by negotiation in advance, and they like to have some security against the chance that you might not pay it back: share certificates or life insurance policies count for this. Overdrafts are a cheap way of borrowing, and partly for this reason banks like to restrict them to three or six months. They prefer to persuade you to take out a *Personal loan*.

Overhead
Your overhead costs are the ones which stay over your head whether your business is busy or idle. Some are more fixed than others: you can lay off some office staff, and even cut your rates if you are not using a factory, but the premises themselves are with you until you sell them.

Over-the-counter market
This is an unofficial stock market. It first sprang up in New York in 1926, where you could buy shares over the counter at a securities house. A version was started in London in

1972 by M. J. H. Nightingale, an investment bank now
called Granville & Co. They buy and sell shares in a small
list of companies which want a *Quote* but also want to keep
an eye on who their shareholders are.

Overtime
This is work done over and above the regular hours laid
down in a *Contract of employment*. It is usually paid for at
a higher rate than the normal hours. In some jobs, overtime
is built into the contract as a regular part of the working
week. Otherwise, it is arranged when the firm needs to clear
a backlog of work. See *Contractual overtime*.

Overtrading
A firm is overtrading if it is taking on more business than
its finances can handle. Trade involves credit, simply
because of the time taken to produce or sell something. An
optimistic businessman may be tempted to take on too
much stock or raw materials in the hope that it will all be
sold at a profit. In that sense, whether a business is
overtrading is a matter of opinion – only finally resolved if
the firm goes bust. See *Overcapitalised, Undercapitalised*.

P45
This is a form issued by the *Inland Revenue*. It is given to
you by your employer when you change jobs, to show your
next employer your *Tax code* and your pay and tax so far in
that *Fiscal year*. It makes it easier to sort out your correct
tax rate. See also *P60, Tax codes*.

P60
This is a form which your employer should give you at the
end of each *Fiscal year*. It shows how much pay you have
received during that year, and what deductions were made.
It is very useful if you have to fill in a *Tax return*, or in the
case of any disputes.

Paid-up policy
This is where you stop paying insurance premiums on a

policy earlier than expected. It is then called a paid-up
policy, and the insurer will tell you how much benefit it will
pay at the end of the period stated in the contract. It can
help you if you need the money for other things, but see
Surrender.

Palanga
The currency of the Tonga Islands in the Pacific. It is worth
about 50p.

Paper money See *Banknote, Money*.

Par
Shares in Britain are normally given a par value for
accountancy purposes. This value, times the number of
shares, is equal to the share capital of a company. If it sells
shares for a higher price, that is put into a share premium
account. The *Dividend* may also be expressed as a percentage
of the par value.

Parity
Parity indicates equality between two different sorts of
prices. A share price is said to be at parity if it is standing at
its *Par* value. Exchange rates are at parity if they accurately
translate prices between two countries. See *Purchasing
power parity*.

Participator
A person with an interest in the capital or income of a *Close
company*, including *Loan creditors*. This applies even if the
interest is held through participating in a company which
in turn controls another company. See *Associates of a
participator*. It can also refer to a licensee of an oil field: see
Petroleum revenue tax.

Partly paid
Some stocks and shares are floated on the stock market
partly-paid. This means that investors have to pay only, say,

25% of the total price initially and the rest later. It is a tactic which is adopted when the securities in question have a large unit value, so that would-be takers are not put off by such a heavy toll on their bank accounts in one go. It also gives the partly-paid securities extra *Gearing*, as they carry the rights to full dividends and the price can therefore go up and down at the full rate. See *Call*.

Partner

A partner is someone who joins with at least one other person to make a profit from some business. There are three types of partner. The first is the full partner. Second is the salaried partner, who gets only a salary, or a salary plus a commission or share of profits. A salaried partner should be careful to define his legal obligations to the firm. Thirdly there are sleeping partners. They put money into a partnership, take no active part, and receive a share of the profits. See *Partnership*.

Partnership

When two or more people work together to produce a profit, they are in partnership. This is a very loose arrangement, and that is reflected in the legal attitude to partnerships, which can be called *Firms*. In essence, the partners are regarded as one person. Income tax is worked out as if they were one, and then divided among the partners. But *Capital Gains Tax* on selling a partnership is assessed individually. Partnerships are ruled by the Partnership Act 1890. See *Partner*.

Pataca

The official currency of Macao, the Portuguese island which faces Hong Kong across the mouth of China's Pearl River. As the only two western tourist spots in the area, Hong Kong and Macao's economies are closely related. Like the Hong Kong dollar, the Pataca is worth about 10p. There are 100 avos to the pataca. On Macao the pataca circulates

side by side with the Hong Kong dollar. The reverse does
not apply in Hong Kong.

Pawnbroker
A dying occupation in this country, mainly because people
do not have as many portable valuables as they used to.
To pawn is to give something as security for a loan, and
pawnbrokers lend against the value of personal possessions
which they can, if necessary, sell. You must pay back within
six months and a day. Although the interest rate may not
be as high as a *Moneylender* may charge, it will still be higher
than on most other forms of borrowing.

Pay As You Earn
This is a scheme to deduct your tax bill before it leaves your
employer each week or month. It means that most people do
not face a horrific amount to pay at the end of each tax year,
and it turns employers into part-time tax collectors. The
tax office inspects your financial position each year, and
assesses how much tax you should pay. He passes the
information on to your employer through a code number.
If you are unhappy about your tax bill, you should get on to
your tax office direct. Your company wages office will know
the address and phone number. See *Tax codes*, *P45*, *P60*.

P/E ratio See *Price/earnings ratio*.

Pecuniary
From the Latin *pecuniarius*, meaning money, pecuniary is
anything relating to money. So 'pecuniary reward' is a
long-winded way of referring to a cash prize. Someone who
is pecunious is simply well-off.

Pecuniary legacy
As its name implies, a pecuniary *Legacy* is a cash gift made
through a *Will*. If the will is not to be paid immediately –
possibly because the beneficiary is a child – the interest on
the money may form part of the legacy. This has to be clearly

stated, or the interest will simply go into the rest of the
Estate.

Penny
A Middle English term, from the same root as the German
Pfennig, which was the label for a small coin and came to
be regularised as one 240th of a pound of silver. See *Denarius*.

Pension
A pension, originally the word for any sort of payment, has
since 1529 referred to a regular income received in
recognition of past services or contributions to an employer
or to the government. And that is very much how it works
today. The State runs a scheme for people who make
National Insurance contributions, and most large companies
run an *Occupational pension* scheme. On top of that, the
self-employed, and those whose firms do not provide, can take
out a plan of their own. See *Additional component*, *Additional
Voluntary Contributions*, *Age Concern*, *Basic component*,
Certificate of age exemption, *Contracting out*, *Earnings related
pensions*, *Invalidity pension*, *Self-employed pensions*, *State
pension*, *Supplementary pension*, *Widow's pension*.

Perfect competition
It cannot exist in practice, but in economic terms perfect
competition is at the other end of the spectrum from *Monopoly*.
It is a starting point for analysing company behaviour. It
assumes that there are an infinite number of fully informed
buyers and sellers in the market, that land, labour and
equipment are mobile and divisible, and the products are
identical. Producers can sell all they make, and if anyone
raises or cuts prices he will be shunned or swamped by
buyers.

Performance fund
The only sort of performance that merits the word in the
investment world is rapid capital growth. A performance fund
should be aggressive, concentrated on a few shares in only

one or two sectors, and pay next to no dividend. If you
take this ride, your payoff comes right at the end, when you
sell for that fat profit the *unit trust* adverts like to hint at.
But beware: high performance can also mean high risk, and
if that is not your style you may suffer sleepless nights.

Permanent health insurance

A slight misnomer, as this is a type of policy designed to
insure people against becoming permanently unhealthy, to the
point where they can no longer work. It seems a remote
chance, but it is reckoned to be more likely than accidental
death. The policy pays an agreed sum per week, and aims
to close the gap between State *Disability benefits* and the
victims' former income. It can be made cheaper by agreeing
to a delay between the onset of the illness and the start of
the payments – many employers will in any case pay a lump
sum of three to six months' wages in such circumstances.
One drawback, though, is that the Inland Revenue may levy
Income Tax on the policy payments after a couple of years.

Personal accident insurance

Also known as public liability insurance, this type of policy
is designed to cover you against one of those freak accidents
which could cost you a lot of money: poking someone's eye
out with an umbrella, or causing a car pile-up by stepping
into the road at the wrong moment. Such accidents could
land you in court for negligence. Because the odds against
a claim are so huge, these policies are very cheap, like
£250,000 for a pound or two of premium. See also *Personal
Liability Insurance, Professional indemnity insurance*.

Personal account

A business opens a personal account for every person or
company that it regularly deals with. The account keeps
a record of those dealings. A special case is the capital
account, which records the owners' investments in the
business.

Personal allowances
These are slices of tax-free income, allowed to individuals
before the taxable income is worked out. If your pay is
£10,000 a year and you have allowances totalling £2,000,
your tax will be worked out on income of £8,000. Everyone
is entitled to at least one personal allowance. The main ones
are the *Single person's*, the *Married man's* and *Child
allowances*, but there are a range of others designed to help
the aged, the disabled and the widowed or separated. Unless
the House of Commons votes otherwise, personal allowances
are adjusted each year in line with the rise in the *Retail
Prices Index* for the year running to the previous
December 31. See also *Age allowance, Death grant,
Disability benefit.*

Personal Equity Plan
A scheme introduced in the 1986 Budget to allow adults to
spend up to £200 a month buying shares. They can be
bought and sold, but the money must stay in a special
account for up to two years, after which all dividends and
capital gains are tax-free. The plan begins in January 1987.

Personal liability insurance
It is very unlikely that you will poke someone in the eye
with an umbrella, but if you do you may be sued for
several thousand pounds. Personal liability insurance pays
on this sort of accidental damage. Because the chances of
a claim are slim, the premium is small. See also *Personal
Accident Insurance.*

Personal loans
These are offered by banks to their personal customers.
They are made for fixed amounts over fixed periods, at a
rate of interest fixed at the start. You probably will not need
collateral to back the loan, but you do have to keep up regular
repayments. From time to time banks are told by the Bank
of England to ration these loans so as to leave more money
available for industry. It is best to take out a personal loan

when interest rates are low. Sadly, you are more likely to
want one when rates are high.

Peseta
As Eva is to Evita, so pesa is to peseta: it is the diminutive
form of the Spanish for pound, and is closely related to the
South American peso. The peseta is the currency of Spain
and its dependencies, including Andorra, the Balearic
Isles, and the Canary Islands. A peseta is worth about ½p.

Peso
The common currency of Spanish South America, although
the value of each national peso has varied widely with their
fluctuating economic fortunes. The most inflated is the
Argentinian australi, which has suffered regular devaluations.
At the other end of the spectrum are the pesos of Cuba and
the Dominican Republic. Other peso nations are Bolivia,
Chile, Colombia, Guinea Bissau, Mexico, Philippines and
Uruguay.

Petrodollar
A combination of petrol and dollar, this is a slang term for
the cash oil-exporting countries have accumulated but have
no immediate use for. Dollars made world currencies
unstable because their owners simply chased the best
return – and ran away from any currency that looked weak,
making it weak in the process. They are called petrodollars
rather than petropounds or petrofrancs because oil is priced
in US dollars.

Petroleum revenue tax
Levied on profits from oil and natural gas drawn from fields
anywhere in the UK or the sea around it. It takes effect when
more than 1,000 tonnes of oil has been extracted, and the
value exceeds the allowable costs. The tax, which took
effect from 12 November 1974, is assessed on each
participator, who include licensees and sub-licensees, in

each field. PRT can be offset against royalty payments, *Corporation tax*, abortive exploration costs and other items.

Petty cash voucher
A voucher vouches that money has been honestly spent. A petty cash voucher can be a shop receipt – or even a bus ticket. Bookkeepers clip them or stick them to a sheet of paper and give them a number for easy reference.

Pfennig
Like the British penny, this comes from the Middle English word *penning*, meaning a small coin. It is now 100th part of a *Mark*.

Piastre
Egypt's minor currency unit. There are 100 to the Egyptian pound.

Piecework
Instead of paying workers by the hour, piecework calculates their pay on the basis of their *Output*. The idea is to encourage workers to work harder, and to give them a sense of the link between their labour and the end result – a saleable product. It is suitable only where each person's output can be easily measured. See *Productivity*.

Pink form See *Preferential form*.

Pit
The pit is an eight-sided area surrounded by a set of steps, on the floor of the *London International Financial Future Exchange*. Here dealings in certain contracts are carried out through *Open outcry*.

Pit broker
A member of the *London International Financial Futures Exchange* who only carries out orders in the *Pit* for other members.

Placing

A private sale of shares in a public company, usually at less than the current stock market price. For this reason, the Stock Exchange tends to frown on placings unless they are a spinoff from another deal, such as a takeover bid, and there is no easy way of offering the shares to existing investors in the company. See *Rights issue*.

Ploughing back

A company ploughs back its profits if it spends them on new equipment or premises instead of distributing them in dividends to shareholders. Most companies try to plough back at least some of their profits each year, but sometimes there is a case for investing the lot: an expansion drive, or a change to new technology. Some companies sweeten shareholders by issuing new shares in place of the 'lost' dividend. The late Frederick Ellis of the *Daily Express* dubbed these 'ploughshares'.

Pluvius

Latin for rain, and the name for a *Weather insurance* policy operated by Eagle Star Insurance.

Point See *Basis point*.

Poisha

The minor currency unit of Bangladesh. There are 100 poisha to the taka. Although they are not worth much, poisha coins circulate in denominations of 5, 10, 25 and 50. See *Taka*.

Policyholders Protection Act

If your insurance firm goes bust, this Act will pay 90% of what you would have been entitled to while your policy stays in force. But that figure is based on only the guaranteed minimum on long-term policies.

Portfolio

A collection of investments in stocks and shares. It derives

from the fact that *Stockbrokers* used to keep records of their
clients' shareholdings in a portfolio or folder. It is also used
to distinguish between buying shares – portfolio
investment – and buying property, factories or whole
businesses – direct investment.

Position
To take or open a position on a market is to make an initial
move, perhaps to buy, perhaps to sell stock you do not have.
When you no longer want to be in that position, you close
it by doing the reverse of your original action: a buyer
sells, and someone who has sold short makes a matching
purchase.

Postal order
If you want to send money through the post, but do not
have a chequebook or fear that cash may be stolen, a postal
order is the answer. You can buy them from a Post Office
in the amount you want, and you write in who can cash
the order and where.

Pound
The British unit of currency, derived from the Roman *libra*,
a measure of weight. Modified down the years, the pound
came into the money game when a pound of silver was taken
as the centre of the British system. Only three other
territories – the Falkland Islands, Gibraltar and St Helena
– now tie their pound to the UK's. Six others still use the
label, although their currencies have floated away. The
Cypriot pound is worth 120p, the Maltese 160p, the
Egyptian 50p, the Sudanese 30p, the Lebanese 5p and the
Syrian 10p.

Pound-cost averaging
A refuge for stockbrokers and unit trust salesmen faced with
angry clients. If you buy a share or a unit at 100 and it falls
to 50, you will be told to relax: pound-cost averaging will
come to your rescue. Buy the same number of shares at

50 and, lo and behold, your average price will have fallen to
only 75. It is a big selling point for regular savings schemes.
Send £100 a month, and if share prices halve your £100 will
buy twice as many! If prices double you will get only half
as many, but you won't mind then because you will be so
pleased to have done so well on what you have already got.
If you feel that pound-cost averaging is a piece of
sleight-of-hand containing a grain of truth, you will not
be far wrong.

Pre-emptive rights
The traditional British system whereby existing shareholders
in a company are normally given the first right to subscribe
for more shares when the company wants to raise fresh
capital. The US custom is to pre-sell the shares to an
investment house which then distributes them wherever it
can. See *Bought deal*.

Preference shares
These are shares which are preferred to a company's ordinary
shares. They have an earlier right to dividends, they are repaid
before ordinary shares in a break-up, and they can have
greater voting power. Preference shares often carry a
guaranteed minimum dividend (assuming there is enough
money to pay it). But there are limited numbers of
preference shares, so they can be difficult to buy or sell.

Preferential form
These are forms sent to employees or existing shareholders
of a company, entitling them to buy new shares at a special
price, or to enable them to jump the queue over outsiders
who may want to apply. Outsiders' forms are on plain
white paper or cut from newspapers, while the preferential
ones are usually pink.

Premium
This is used in both the stock market and insurance. An
insurance premium is the regular sum you pay on a policy.

A loan stock is at a premium if its market value is above its
nominal or par value. It is a way of saying that the value
of an asset has gone up.

Premium Bond
This is a British compromise on the national lotteries which
do so well on the continent. Nearly half the population owns
at least one Premium Bond. They pay no guaranteed
interest, but go into a draw every month which pays prizes
from £50 to £250,000. The prize money comes from the
interest which would otherwise have been handed out. The
quickness of the hand deceives the eye: while the bond
holders hope they will win a fortune, the rate of interest has
always lagged behind market rates. See *Ernie*, *National
Savings*.

Pre-Retirement Association of Great Britain and Northern Ireland
Based at 19 Undine Street, Tooting, London SW17 8PP,
this body aims to help people prepare for retirement
through publications, courses and an information service.
See *Age Concern*, *Employment Fellowship* and *Help the
Aged*.

Prevention of Fraud (Investments) Act
The Act which gives the Department of Trade and Industry
responsibility for supervising *Unit trusts*, *Investment trusts* and
Licensed dealers.

Price
A price tells you what you have to give up to receive a
particular item or service. In a money society, prices are
usually expressed in terms of money. But there is nothing
to stop a buyer and seller agreeing to price something more
directly, by bartering.

Price/earnings ratio
An American import, the p/e ratio is a way of comparing

share prices. It is simply a company's share price divided
by its earnings per share. The higher the result, the dearer
the share price. A p/e ratio of 2 or 3 suggests that the stock
market is taking very little on trust. But if a firm's p/e is
over 30, it is clearly regarded as a growth stock. The share
price list on the inside back pages of the *Financial Times*
shows the p/e of each company, and on a nearby page
there is a table of averages to compare them with. But if you
wish to calculate p/e ratios for yourself, note that the
definition of company earnings has been complicated by the
birth of *Imputation tax* in 1973.

Primary dealer
The Wall Street term for a *market maker* in the US Treasury
Bond market, the equivalent of the British gilt-edged
market.

Primary market
From the point of view of dealers on a *Futures* market, the
primary market is the one which deals in the underlying
securities or commodities. For the *London International
Financial Futures Exchange*, the primary market may be
the *Foreign exchange* market, the money market, or the *Stock
Exchange*.

Prime costs
This is one of the two main categories in a set of
Manufacturing accounts. It covers *Direct expenses* like raw
materials. The prime cost section then goes forward to the
Cost of manufactured goods section, which adds the prime
costs to *Overheads* and *Work in progress*.

Prime rate
This is the term used in US banking for the lowest rate of
interest a bank is willing to charge borrowers. It is the rate
paid by the highest-grade borrowers, and all others are
graded up from that.

Principal Registry
Officially part of the Family Division of the High Court,
this is where *Wills* are registered. It is also the body which
formally grants *Probate* on wills. The probate personal
application department is at Golden Cross House,
Duncannon Street, London WC2N 4JF.

Prior charges
Before a company can pay a dividend to shareholders, it
usually has to meet other financial obligations. There is a
strict pecking order, led by holders of *Debentures*, *Mortgages*,
Loans and *Preference shares*. Interest or dividends due on
any of these are a prior charge as far as the shareholder is
concerned.

Private company See *Public limited company*.

Private enterprise
Enterprise carried on by private firms or individuals, as
opposed to government-owned corporations or
organisations, such as nationalised industries.

Private sector See *Public sector*.

Probate
Probate, or, more properly, grant of probate, is a legal term
for the official agreement by the Principal Registry (Family
Division) of the High Court that a *Will* is genuine, or proved.
Without that agreement, the *Executor* is not allowed to
start disposing of the property in the dead person's *Estate*.

Probate price
When a shareholder dies, his investments have to be valued
for *Probate* purposes, and to decide any tax liability such as
Inheritance Tax. The price is taken from the Stock Exchange
Official List on the relevant date. The list quotes a buying
and a selling price for each *Security*. The formula, known as
the quarter-up principle, is to divide the difference by
four, and add the result to the lower of the two prices.

Probate prices valuation
When a will is being proved, the non-money assets in the
estate must be valued, both for tax and to decide how it should
be divided among the beneficiaries. Stocks and shares are
valued on a traditional formula based on the prices in the
Stock Exchange Daily Official List on the day of death (see
Probate price).

Production
To the economist, the creation of anything useful counts as
production, whether it is goods or services. The test is
whether anyone will pay for it.

Productivity
The productivity of a factor of production is how much it
produces in a given span. It is used most controversially
in regard to labour, but can also be applied to equipment or
land.

Profession
Much grander than a *Trade*, a profession classically involves
acquiring a body of knowledge through study, and then
earning a living by charging fees for professing that
knowledge. It used to refer only to the professions of the
law, medicine and religion. Now many white-collar
occupations are claimed as professions, and a professional
has been warped to mean almost anyone who is good at his
job.

Professional and Executive Recruitment
Part of the *Manpower Services Commission*, PER is a free
service to people seeking professional or management jobs.
As well as offering advice and special courses, PER maintains
its own register of jobs, and screens candidates for
interview. Your local *Job Centre* will refer you automatically
to PER if it thinks that they will have your sort of job. PER
has offices throughout the country. Its base is at 4 Grosvenor
Place, London SW1.

Professional indemnity insurance
An insurance policy to protect you against causing loss or
damage to anyone else through your job. It is called
'professional' because it is largely aimed at doctors and
lawyers, but anyone can have one. The main insurers of
this type of risk are at Lloyd's. They will want extensive
details of the particular business being insured, so that
they can assess the risk. See also *Personal accident insurance*,
Personal liability insurance.

Profit
At its simplest, it is the difference between what you pay
for something and what you get for selling it. For a business,
profit is the annual turnover or sales, minus the annual costs.
But how costly are the costs? You buy raw or half-finished
materials, you pay the workers, the fuel bills, the council
rates. But what about your equipment? It is bound to have
got worn down a little. It may be that your deadliest rival
has a new machine so good that all yours might as well be
thrown away. And what about that shifty-looking customer
you have not seen for a year – will he ever pay you? If not,
that's part of your profit out of the window.

Profit margin
In trading terms, the profit margin is the difference between
the prices a firm buys and sells at. Shopkeepers in
particular add a set percentage to their buying price. This
should cover their overheads – rent, power, wages – and
of course leave something over for themselves. The profit
margin is also commonly known as the mark-up. If the
margin has been correctly calculated, at the end of each year
it should yield a *Trading profit*.

Progressive tax
A politically loaded term for taxes which are loaded so that
the richer pay proportionately more and the poorer
proportionately less – with the hope that this bias will be
reinforced by spending more of the subsequent revenue

on the poorer. A classic example has been income tax, which takes an increasing percentage of successively higher slices of income.

Project Fullemploy
This is a charity backed by a huge list of City and industrial companies as well as local authorities, with the aim of training and finding work for 'unqualified, untrained and unemployed' young people. It runs a series of full-time courses which give youngsters practical experience on the job and at special centres. The project is monitored by the *Manpower Services Commission*. Project Fullemploy's address is c/o Bates, Wells and Braithwaite, Fleur-de-Lys House, 81 Carter Lane, London EC4V 5EP.

Promissory note
This is a grand name for what is generally called an IOU. It is a written and signed promise to pay a certain sum to an agreed person on an agreed day. It can be traded. See *Bill of exchange, Commercial bill, Fine trade bill*.

Prospectus
The document through which promoters of a stock or share give the public details of the company whose securities are being offered, and the terms of the offer. See also *Red Herring*.

Protectionism
The 'ism' that imposes *Tariffs* on certain imports to protect a home industry. If a country establishes a sudden lead in a new industry, such as computers, other countries may throw up a tariff to give themselves time to compete. It can be a defence against *Dumping* and may help save jobs. But it is always open to retaliation, and the *General Agreement on Tariffs and Trade* is committed to discouraging the practice.

Prudential Assurance
Britain's biggest insurance and pensions company, with an

imposing red-brick head office in Holborn, London EC1.
Although it is best known to the public for the *Man from
the Pru* knocking on people's doors, in recent years the huge
amounts of money flowing into the Pru from pensions and
insurance premiums have turned the company into one of
the biggest investors in the country too. The figures are
changing all the time, but the Pru has been estimated to
own 3% of all the shares traded on the Stock Exchange, as
well as millions of pounds of *Gilts*. The Pru is also a major
owner of property. From the policyholder's point of view,
though, its record is solid rather than spectacular. See
Insurance and *Home service insurance*.

Public finance
The management of money and resources by central and
local government. It is a question of how tax revenue and
borrowing should be used to meet political spending
objectives.

Public liability insurance See *Personal accident insurance*.

Public limited company
The 1980 Companies Act introduced the notion of a public
limited company, or plc, to conform with the European
Community's second directive on company law. A plc must
state that it is so in its *Memorandum of association*, must
have at least two members, and must have a nominal share
capital of at least £50,000. Of that sum, at least a quarter,
or £12,500, must be paid up. Only plc's can offer their
shares to the public. Any limited company which does not
qualify as a plc is a private company.

Public loss assessor
Many insurance policyholders are frightened off by the
forms needed to make a claim, and are worried that they might
lose money on some obscure technicality. A public loss
assessor is hired by the policyholder to represent his interests
and see him through the legal minefield. There is an Institute

of Public Loss Assessors. It has about 200 members and
sets standards of qualification and conduct. Its address is 14
Red Lion Street, Chesham, Buckinghamshire. See also
Insurance, Loss adjuster.

Public sector
This is central and local government, nationalised industries,
public corporations and the issue department of the *Bank of
England*. This is what the Chancellor of the Exchequer is
referring to when he talks about how much the public sector
will be spending in the next year. The private sector is, in
effect, everything else, including individuals and
companies. See also *Public Sector Borrowing Requirement*.

Public Sector Borrowing Requirement
Technically, this need have nothing to do with borrowing:
it just usually works out that way. In terms of government
accounting, it is the difference, or balance, between the
Public sector's income and spending. Occasionally, as in
1969, this has been in surplus. Monetarists believe that it is
a major engine of *Inflation*. Their opponents believe it can
be a major engine of new employment.

Public Works Loans Board
A lender of last resort to local authorities. Funded by the
government, this board will lend to councils which are
suddenly short of cash, or cannot borrow from other
sources.

Pula
The main currency of Botswana, between Angola and South
Africa. It is worth about 40p.

Punt
This is the Irish Republic's translation of the pound. Until
1978, because of the close economic links, the Irish pound
was tied to the British one. But then the Irish broke away,
renaming their unit at the same time. It is now worth only
about 90% of the UK pound.

Purchase
To acquire or gain possession of something, other than by inheriting or stealing it. And in this hard world, that usually means giving money in exchange for it. In that sense, purchase has become synonymous with *Buy*.

Purchasing power parity
If foreign exchange markets are operating freely, given amounts of different currencies should in theory be able to buy the same amount of goods. If £1 equals 10 French francs, a loaf costing 30p in England should cost 3fr. in France. But a French loaf is not like a British one, and sudden crises can distort exchange rates. It is a reasonable long-term guideline, though.

Put See *Option*.

Pya
The minor Burmese coin, counting as 100th of a kyat. Pya coins are issued in denominations of one to 50.

Pyramid selling
A practice, now outlawed, in which a sales operation was run like a chain letter. The man at the top would recruit senior salesmen, who would pay for the stock they were to sell. This gave them the incentive to find the next rung of salesmen to pass the goods on to – at a profit, of course. The system spread out and worked its way down to the people who might pay several hundred pounds for goods they were supposed to sell door-to-door. Inevitably, some of those near the bottom of the pyramid lost money.

Pyramiding
This is a stock market tactic, to keep buying a share whose price is rising. See *Pound cost averaging*.

Qualifying loan or policy
These are *Loans* or *Insurance* policies which qualify for *Tax*

relief. To do so, they have to meet standards laid down by law and monitored by the Inland Revenue. Insurance companies normally make sure that they sell policies which qualify, but you must check carefully yourself to find out whether the interest you pay on a loan will be allowable against tax. The rules change constantly, but they generally have to do with property or *Inheritance Tax* payments.

Quantity theory of money

A much-respected truism in economics. It states that the amount of money in an economy, times the speed or velocity at which it circulates, is equal to the level of prices times the number of transactions or trades. It was reduced by Fisher early in this century to the equation $MV = PT$. It has become fashionable again with the revival of *Monetarism*, as it can give clues to the rate of *Inflation*.

Quarter-up See *Probate price*.

Queen's Award for Industry

On the theory that the honours system makes people work harder, in 1965 a parallel scheme was launched to award companies for success in either exporting or developing new technology. Interested companies should apply to the Queen's Award Office, Dean Bradley House, Horseferry Road, London SW1.

Quetzal

The currency of Guatemala, in Central America. It is tied to the US dollar.

Quick ratio

Another term for *Acid test*.

Quota

A way of curbing imports by putting a physical limit on the amount of certain types of goods which may enter the country. This can be expensive to administer and police,

and naturally causes resentment among the exporters of
the goods which have been placed under quota.

Quotation See *Quote*.

Quote
Quoted companies have share quotes. This means that the
price of their shares or, for that matter, loan stock and
Debentures is quoted on the Stock Exchange whenever
anyone wants to know it. In practice, you can find the current
quote for most shares on the stock market in the back pages
of the *Financial Times*. But see *Middle price*.

Rack rent
Using 'rack' in its medieval sense, to stretch, a rack rent is
a rent which is stretched to the full. The formal definition is
a rent which is equal to the full annual value of the property,
but it has become identified with the idea of an extortionate
or penal rent.

Rally
An upturn in prices on a market. It is similar to a *Recovery*.
A rally is often a sharper rise, but perhaps more
short-lived.

Rand
South Africa's currency, worth about 30p. Also used by the
South West African Territories, or Namibia. The Swazi
lilangeni is tied to the rand.

Rate
A tax levied by local authorities on residents and companies
in the area. The amount to be paid depends on the size, quality
and position of property owned. Each property is given a
rateable value, which is then linked to the rate which the
council declares it is charging on that value, at so much in
the pound. If a building is valued at £1,000 and the rate
is £1.50 in the pound, the payment will be £1,500 a year.

Rateable value
This is the value of a property for the purpose of deciding how much *Rate* the occupants should pay. It is calculated by taking the *Gross value* and subtracting the estimated yearly cost of repairs.

Rate support grant
This is a grant given by central government to local authorities, to help them bridge any gap between their spending and their income from rates. Under the Local Government, Planning and Land Act 1980, the Secretary of State for the Environment can decide how much a local authority can spend per head of population, and therefore how large its rate support grant should be.

REACH See *Retired Executives Action Clearing House.*

Reaction
A fall in market prices, following directly on from a *Recovery*. In that sense, prices are said to be reacting to the previous increase.

Real account
A bookkeeping term for the accounts a business keeps of its real assets: cash, bank deposits, furniture, motor vehicles, land and buildings. You debit a real account when its value rises, because it has had money spent on it. You credit the account when its value falls, because the asset has given up some of its value to the business.

Real income
What your wages will buy, ignoring the effects of inflation. It is generally used in comparisons, either among wages in different companies or industries, or among wages paid in similar jobs over a period of years. *Inflation* makes wage increases look higher than they are, so that part is deducted and what is left is the rise in the real income.

Rebate

A rebate is a repayment or a discount on a sum of money
that you owe. It can be paid by a trader if you buy in bulk
from him, but it is more often used to refer to repayments
of tax, rates or rent. A tax rebate is paid if the Inland
Revenue reckons that you have paid too much in the past.
Rate and rent rebates are paid by local councils to the
needy, depending on your income and the size of your
family. Your council will give you a leaflet setting out the
rules.

Receipt

A receipt is a proof of payment, when a debtor has paid a
debt. It is in that sense the counterpart of the *Invoice*.
Under the Cheques Act 1957, if payment is made by cheque
a receipt does not have to be issued.

Receiver

A receiver is an accountant who is appointed by creditors,
often with the approval of the courts, to take charge of a
company and receive enough of its assets to pay those
creditors without necessarily liquidating the company. He
is sometimes called a receiver and manager, because his job
is usually to manage the company as a going concern,
leaving enough money in the business to let it trade, but
extracting his employers' cash whenever he can. However,
he may recommend that there is no alternative to a complete
breakup. See *Liquidator*

Receiving order

A court order giving the *Official Receiver* the right to seize
a debtor's assets. He will sell as much of them as he needs
to pay off the debts. If these sales are not enough, the debtor
is declared *Bankrupt*.

Recession

This is literally the act of receding, or giving up previous
gains. It was adopted by economists in the 1960s to describe

a slowing down in the economy, short of a full-blown *Slump*. Inevitably it became devalued into a weasel-word by politicians who did not want to admit that their voters were in a *Depression*. See also *Boom*, *Trade cycle*.

Recognised bank
The *Banking Act 1979* created two categories of firms allowed to take deposits from the public. The first is the recognised bank, which must have 'a high reputation and standing in the financial community' and either provide a wide range of banking services, or a highly specialised service. See *Licensed deposit-taker*.

Recognised Clearing House
Another creation of the Financial Services Act, it will serve a *Recognised Investment Exchange* with facilities for settling and clearing transactions.

Recognised Investment Exchange
Recognised under the Financial Services Act, an RIE will offer investors an approved standard of supervised trading facilities, and will publish prices for all to see.

Recommended retail price
Since *Resale Price Maintenance* was abolished in 1964, most manufacturers have been forbidden from forcing retailers to sell their goods at a certain price. Instead, they are allowed only to recommend a price, which the shopkeeper may or may not follow, as he sees fit. This was intended to increase competition and help the consumer. Some shops now advertise their wares in terms of how much they are knocking off the recommended price. However, some goods like books and newspapers are still sold under the old rules.

Recoverable amount
An accounting term. It means what you can sell an asset for, or how much you can make out of using it.

Recovery
A broadly based rise in market prices, usually from what have been thought of as depressed levels. See *Rally*, *Reaction*.

Redeemable
Anything which can be bought back for cash is redeemable. Typical is a *Gilt* or a company *Loan stock*, where a date for redemption is given at the outset. The fur coat which you take to a pawnbroker is also redeemable.

Redemption See *Redeemable*.

Redemption yield
The *Yield* from a fixed interest stock, including gains made on the price at which you buy and sell the stock itself. See *Flat yield*.

Red herring
A preliminary *prospectus* for a company share issue, giving details of the company and its prospects, but not containing a price for the shares. It is used to test the market's reaction, and so hopefully price the issue more accurately.

Rediscount
Commercial bills, originally sold by the creditor at a discount, are then rediscounted as they are traded round the *Discount market*.

Redundancy
You are redundant if you have been dismissed because your employer is closing or moving the part of the business you were working on, or if your type of work is being phased out. Under the Employment Protection (Consolidation) Act 1978, that is the definition of redundancy which entitles unemployed people to the *Statutory redundancy payment*, if they have done two years' continuous service. See also *Dismissal*, *Redundancy notice*, *Redundancy fund*.

Redundancy fund

This is a State-run fund drawn from the money employers pay under the Social Security Act. It is used to make it easier for companies to declare redundancies, in that they can then claim a rebate from the fund. This may help the company to survive, protecting the jobs of those who stay on.

Redundancy notice

Redundant workers are entitled to the same period of notice as anyone else who is dismissed: a week if you have worked for the company for four weeks or more, and then a week's notice for every year of service after two years. The firm must also give a consultation period before any redundancies are declared, 30 days if 10–99 employees are affected, 90 days if more than 100 employees are to go. Anyone made redundant is entitled to time off to look for another job. See *Length of service*.

Redundancy payment

This is money paid to you by your employer when you are made redundant. It is usually equal to the pay you would have received during the *Notice period* laid down in your *Contract of employment*. There may be a bonus on top of that if your boss is feeling generous or thinks he may need you again in future. At present, the first £25,000 of a redundancy cheque should be tax-free. If you get more than that, ask the advice of a tax expert.

Re-export

Many goods are imported into Britain only to be exported, often after they have been used in production. They are called re-exports.

Reflation

This is a deliberate act by the government to stimulate the economy, usually by pumping in more money to encourage demand and production.

Regional development grant

If you spend money on a building, mining work or new plant or machinery in certain designated areas you can get a cash grant under the Industry Act 1972. No matter how much grant you receive, you still collect a *First year allowance* on the total cost.

Registered office

By law, every limited company has to put on public file an address which counts as its registered office. The company name has to be displayed outside the premises, which prevents firms from dreaming up an address or using one without the owner's permission. The registered office makes it easier for anyone to get in touch with the company. The addresses are lodged at *Companies House*, which has offices in Cardiff, Edinburgh and London.

Regressive tax

A tax which has a relatively harsher effect on the poorer than the richer taxpayer. An obvious example is a flat-rate tax of £5 on a bottle of whisky. This is a bigger proportion of the income of a £5,000-a-year earner than someone on £20,000 a year.

Regulated tenancy

A regulated tenancy is a home which has a registered *Fair rent*. Under the 1980 Housing Act, this term replaced the former controlled tenancy. See also *Assured tenancy*, *Shorthold tenancy*, *Tenant*.

Reinsurance

Insurers hate to be thought of as bookmakers, but they lay their bets off all the same. Even a big insurer who bets that a tanker will not sink, or 100,000 houses will not crumble under a harsh winter, can be horribly exposed if things go wrong. So he goes to a reinsurer, who takes on a little of many insurers' risks. Just to complicate matters, some insurance companies do a little reinsurance too. The top

reinsurers are Swiss Re and Munich Re, who operate wide
intelligence networks to make sure they hear bad news
before anyone else – and adjust their rates accordingly.

Relief See *Tax relief*.

Remploy
A State-run industrial concern devoted to employing
disabled people. It was founded under the Disabled
Persons (Employment) Act 1944 as the Disabled Persons
Employment Corporation. Remploy makes furniture,
packaging, leather and textiles. It has a board appointed by
the Secretary of State for Employment, and its policies are
laid down by the *Manpower Services Commission*. Remploy
is based at 415 Edgware Road, London NW2 6LR. See
also *Disabled*.

Remuneration certificate
If you are unhappy with a solicitor's bill, you can ask him
to obtain a remuneration certificate from the *Law Society*.
The Society either issues a certificate, confirming that the
bill is reasonable, or orders it to be reduced. If you pay a
solicitor's bill straight off, you lose the right to a
remuneration certificate.

Renminbi
The Chinese word for its currency, as distinct from its main
currency unit, the yuan.

Rent allowance
This is the alternative to *Rent rebates* for tenants in private
housing. While a council can give a rebate simply by cutting
the rent in an individual case, it is easier to give private
tenants a cash sum to help them pay their landlord. The
money comes from the council just the same, and the *Tenant*
has to show he or she has difficulties paying. Tenants on
Supplementary benefit get an addition to that instead of the
allowance.

Rent pooling

This is the system which local authorities use to work out rents for council housing in their area on a consistent basis. Every house has a *Gross value*. The total gross values on all the houses is set against the total net outgoings, after allowing for any subsidies. If £50m a year is being spent, and the gross values total £40m, then if rents are set at 1.25 times gross value the income and expenditure will match. Many councils have refinements on this theme.

Rent rebate

This is a cut in the rent council tenants have to pay. It is decided on the basis of a means test. The 'needs' of each size of family are worked out and compared with the actual family's income. If the two match, the *Tenant* pays only 40 per cent of the rent. If the income is more than the official 'need' figure, the tenant pays 40 per cent of the rent, plus 17p out of every pound by which the income tops the 'need'. If income is less than 'need', the tenant will pay less than 40 per cent of the rent, down to zero if necessary. See *Unified housing benefit, Rent allowance*.

Renunciation

Renunciation means surrendering or giving up. This is what you can do when you receive an *Allotment letter* allocating you some shares. There is a renunciation period during which you can sell the shares without paying *Stamp duty* and other fees.

Repair grant

This is one of a range of *Housing grants* given by local councils. The repair grant means what it says, and it is designed for repairs to houses in derelict areas, or those built before 1919. See *Improvement grant, Special grant*.

Replacement cost

This is the cost of replacing an asset used in a business. It is an important part of accountancy, as an accurate estimate

of replacement helps to determine how much profit a
business is really making. But there is more than one way
to skin a cat: see *Gross current replacement cost, Net replacement
cost*.

Resale price maintenance
Given their head, there is nothing manufacturers like better
than total control of absolutely everything. And what more
important than to control the prices shopkeepers charge the
public for your goods? Such control can stop *Dumping*,
but in practice it protected the inefficient shop from
competition. It was outlawed in 1964, except for a small
list of exempt goods such as books and newspapers.

Reserve currency
As countries have varying degrees of trust in one another's
currencies, it is convenient to be able to use a currency in
international trade which everyone feels happy with. Thanks
to our former empire, the pound used to have this role,
but it has been largely supplanted by the US dollar. A
reserve currency has to be in plentiful supply, have a stable
value and be backed by a sophisticated banking system back
home.

Reserves
These are the bottom drawer of a company or a government.
Companies try to build up reserves of past profits to meet
sudden needs or pay for expansion. Governments keep
reserves of gold and foreign exchange to finance trade and
defend their own currency on foreign exchange markets.

Residuary legacy
A residuary legacy is what's left over after all the other
Legacies and *Devises* have been handed out under the terms
of a *Will*, as well as the executor's expenses and any *Capital
Transfer Tax*.

Resistance level
A *Chart* term describing a price for a share which has recently

acted as a ceiling or floor for the trend. It suggests to the chartist that there has been a pool of ready buyers at the lower resistance level – or ready sellers at the higher level. If the trend breaks through a resistance level, it is seen as an omen that the price is going to go hurtling onwards in the same direction for some distance before stopping.

Restrictive Practices Court
A part of the High Court designed to adjudge restrictive trade agreements referred to it by the *Office of Fair Trading*. Such deals are restrictive unless proved otherwise by passing through one of a series of 'gateways' allowing that if the agreement were scrapped it would deny benefits to the public, injure them, cut exports, employment or research, raise prices or weaken the fight against a monopoly.

Retail
This comes from the Old French *retaille*, meaning a piece cut off, and was first used in Britain to refer to the business of selling things in small quantities. Before long, it became identified with shopkeeping. Lately, though, the early meaning has been revived by a division of banking into *Wholesale* and retail – the latter describing the handling of small amounts of money for the public, as opposed to wholesale banking with industry.

Retail banking
This is a piece of jargon referring to the side of banking concerned with the public through the bank branches. It includes all the consumer services such as cheques, credit cards, personal loans and small company finance. The big stuff is called *Wholesale banking*.

Retail prices index
This index is the yardstick for calculations of the rate of *Inflation*. It is calculated monthly and issued by the Department of Employment. The raw material comes from civil servants buying a set basket of goods which are

reckoned to be on the shopping list of the 'average' family.
The list is changed occasionally to take account of social
trends and improvements in the goods. It also includes
housing costs. See *Tax* and *Prices index*.

Retention pay
When redundancies have been declared, it can happen that
the employer wants everyone to stay on as long as possible –
perhaps to finish a big order. To stop the leavers from going
off to new jobs immediately, the firm may offer retention pay
in the form of a lump sum or a bonus per shift – to be paid
right at the end.

Retired Executives Action Clearing House
A charity designed to put retired managers in touch with
voluntary bodies needing the help of people with executive
skills. Its address is Victoria House, Southampton Row,
London WC1B 4DH.

Return on assets
This is a method of gauging how well a business is
performing. The *Assets* in this case are defined as the issued
share capital, loan capital, reserves, deferred tax and
minority interests added together, minus any intangibles
such as *Goodwill*. The return is the company's pre-tax profits
plus any interest payable on loan stocks, and this is worked
out as a percentage of the assets.

Revaluation
A more elegant way of saying 'upvaluation', for a currency
which is appreciating. It is effectively the opposite of
Devaluation. A currency is revalued when foreign exchange
dealers expect that country's interest rates to rise, or its prices
to fall, relative to others.

Revaluation method
Some assets *Depreciate* in unpredictable ways, particularly
if they are property, livestock or a machine which is about to

be overtaken by a new technology. In these cases, it is
unrealistic to stick to a mathematical formula. Instead they
can simply be valued from time to time by an independent
valuer. See *Diminishing balance method*, *Straight line
method*.

Revenue deficit subsidy

This is a payment by the government to a *Housing association*
which is short of money on its regular outgoings. This is
particularly liable to happen in the early days of an
association, before rents begin to flow.

Reverse head and shoulders See *Head and shoulders*.

Reverse yield gap

Until the 1950s, the *Yield* from shares was always higher
than on *Gilts*, reflecting the view that shares were riskier. But
as inflation took hold, investors realised that fixed-interest
stocks would not withstand the fall in the value of money.
Shares, however, could benefit from the paper profits that
companies could earn from being able to raise their prices
more easily. The risk in *Equities* appeared to shrink. The
result was that the traditional yield gap was reversed, and gilts
yielded more than shares.

Rial

One of a family of Arab currencies whose name means
'royal'. The rial is used in Iran, where there are about 120
to the pound, and the Sultanate of Oman – where one rial
is worth £1.70. See also ryal.

Riel

The currency of Kampuchea, also known as Kambuja or
Srok Khmer – the South-east Asian country which until
1975 was called Cambodia. For some time after that the only
currency which foreigners could use was the US dollar,
but a domestic currency has been slowly reintroduced.

Right to buy
Under the 1980 Housing Act, tenants who have been in a
council house for at least three years can apply to buy it. It
must not, however, be specially designated for old people.
The buyers can get a discount on the market value of the
house, rising from 33% for a three-year tenant to 50% for
tenants of 20 years and over, so long as it is not less than
the cost of providing the house. This makes a difference
with new houses. Your council can give full details, the
Citizens' Advice Bureau may be able to help, and the
Department of the Environment can send you form RTBI.
It is a good idea to get legal advice early on.

Rights issue
When a company wants to raise more money without
borrowing it, new shares can be created and offered to
existing shareholders. This is called a rights issue, because
the shareholders are entitled to buy them as of right. To
make the new shares more attractive, they are priced at
about 20% less than the current market value. This can
give an added worth to the existing shares until they go
'ex-rights', when buying them will no longer entitle
investors to take part in the rights issue. But often the first
reaction is to mark the price down because the shares are
about to lose some scarcity value – and the market is
suspicious of firms which cannot generate enough cash
from their own day-to-day business.

Ringgit
The currency of Malaysia, the ringgit was formerly called a
dollar, as are those of its neighbours, Singapore and
Brunei. Although there are no formal ties, all three
currencies are valued at about the same, around three to the
pound. The ringgit is still divided into 100 cents.

Road Traffic Act insurance See *Motor insurance*.

Rouble
Dating from 1554, the rouble is the currency of the Union

of Soviet Socialist Republics and stems from the Russian
word 'rubli', meaning 'a piece cut off'. There are 100 kopeks
to the rouble, which is officially worth about 90p. It is
believed to be worth considerably less in illegal black-market
transactions.

Round tripping
A type of *Arbitrage* on the money market. For brief periods,
interest rates can get out of line so that it is possible to
borrow from a bank on *Overdraft* and lend the money on to
the money market – where the same bank may be forced
to borrow it back to balance its books. This is more liable
to happen when there is a fixed *Bank rate* set by the Bank
of England.

Roup
A Scottish and north of England word for an *Auction*. It
comes from a Scandinavian word meaning to shout or
brag.

Royal Institution of Chartered Suryeyors
This is the main body of surveyors in Britain. If your estate
agent or house surveyor has the letters FRICS or ARICS
after his or her name, you can be assured of a good
professional standard – and you can always complain to
the Institution if you are unhappy. Its head office is at 12
Great George Street, London SW1P 3AD. See also
Surveyors.

Royalty
A method of paying artists and authors for the use of their
copyright in a work, by giving them a proportion of every
copy sold. It may be a percentage or a cash sum per copy.
The royal element stemmed from the payment to the
monarch in recognition of his royal rights over a plot of
land.

Rufiyaa
As the Maldive Islands, off the southern tip of India, have

become a tourist centre in their own right, so they have
developed a more distinctive currency. The rufiyaa is a
recent renaming of what was the Maldive rupee, and is
worth about 10p in the shops of Male, the capital. There is
also an official rate valuing the rufiyaa at double the shop
rate. In the outer islands of the Maldive chain, the rufiyaa
is still vying with the US dollar as the main currency.

Run on a bank
When people are worried that a bank might collapse, they
really do run to it to get their money out. Banks always fear
rumours of a run, for the fact is that none of them could
pay all their depositors in cash at once. They rely on being
able to lend on the money that is left with them, and try to
keep their cash in the tills as low as they can get away
with. Normally this works smoothly . . . until the rumours
begin.

Rupee
The currency of the Indian subcontinent, still used by its
now separate parts. The rupee used to be divided into 16
annas, but it has been decimalised into 100 paise – except
in Sri Lanka, which has 100 cents to its rupee. The Bhutan
ngultrum is tied to the rupee at some 17 to the pound. The
Seychelles version is only 9 to a pound, while in Mauritius
it is 19, Nepal and Pakistan 24, and Sri Lanka 40.

Rupiah
The currency unit of Indonesia, and it is liable to rapid falls
in value.

Ryal
Like its Arab cousin the rial, this is the local equivalent of
'royal'. It is used in three countries, Qatar, Saudi Arabia and
North Yemen. Each has a different value, but they are all
worth between 10p and 20p.

Salary
Originally, this was merely the money given to Roman

soldiers for them to buy salt. However, the Latin gloss
gave the word a snobbish appeal, and it has come to refer
to the monthly pay of office workers. See *Wage*.

Salary sacrifice

As you pay the highest rate of tax on the top slice of your
income, anything which cuts that slice off is worth
considering. Salary sacrifice does just that, and puts the
money you surrender into an insurance policy giving tax
benefits and an investment return. As a way of topping up
your pension rights, it is an alternative to *Additional
voluntary contributions* – but it needs the co-operation of your
employer, and any future employer.

Sale

There was a far-off time when a sale was simply the word
to describe the act of selling, when a thing or service was
swopped for money. Then one day a store announced that
it was holding a cut-price sale of shelf-hardened stock, and
life was never the same again. The public flocked, the
shopkeepers rubbed their hands, and an industry was
born. Now goods are brought in specially for the twice-yearly
sales and the game is played to a fat book of rules. See
Office of Fair Trading.

Sale of Goods Act 1893 (updated 1979)

The basis of present-day *Consumer law*. It lays down that
goods for sale must be described accurately, must be in
reasonable condition and must be capable of being used for
the purpose intended. For the first time, it put the onus
on the seller of the goods, stopping him from passing the
buck to the manufacturer – who might be foreign, have
changed his address or be out of business by then. However,
the Act gives only limited protection if the seller is a
private individual. Other loopholes have been closed by
recent legislation. See *Consumer law*.

Samurai bond See *Bulldog bond*.

Satang
Thailand's minor currency unit. There are 100 satang to one
baht.

Save As You Earn.
You see, Whitehall does have a sense of humour. Knowing
that taxpayers dreaded the initial PAYE – for Pay As You
Earn – the civil servants thought up SAYE for the National
Savings monthly index-linked savings plan. It was
introduced in 1975 alongside *Granny bonds*. The grannies
were allowed to have a lump sum index-linked, but everyone
else was restricted to index-linking a steady trickle of savings
from their pay packet. The inflation-proofing effect begins
only as each instalment is invested in SAYE. The contract
lasts five years, and there is an option to leave the money
in for a further two years, when it earns a bonus and
effectively becomes the same as an *Index-linked certificate*.
Building societies operate a similar scheme.

Scalp
A verb used on financial markets, meaning to try and create
small, short-term profits by opening and closing a *Position*
within a few minutes or at most a few hours.

Schedule A
This is an Inland Revenue tax schedule. It covers profits
from rent on land and buildings in the United Kingdom.

Schedule B
The tax schedule relating to income from commercially-run
woodlands in the United Kingdom. The tax is worked out
at one-third the value of the land.

Schedule C
This is a tax schedule which applies if a bank or other agent
receives interest on *Gilt*-edged stock and deducts the tax

before passing what's left on to the owner of the stock. If the owner collects the interest direct, the tax is worked out under Schedule D.

Schedule D
This covers income tax on the profits of trades, professions and anything which does not come under the other schedules, such as income from foreign investments or interest paid *Gross*.

Schedule E
This is the popular income tax schedule, in that most people come under it. Schedule E relates to tax on wages, salaries, commissions, bonuses – anything stemming from employment.

Schedule F
Tax on company dividends, paid under the *Imputation* system, falls under this Inland Revenue schedule.

Schilling
The Austrians' main currency unit. Deriving from a German term of 1693, but ultimately stemming from the Old English *scilling*. There are 100 groschen to the modern schilling, which is in turn worth about 3p.

School costs
Many parents can get help with the cost of sending children to school. Local education authorities pay fares if a child lives far enough away from the school. Parents receiving *Supplementary benefit* or *Family income supplement* can get free school meals for their children. Some local education authorities give grants for clothing, and also to boost the family income so that 16-year-olds can stay at school.

School fees insurance
These come in various guises, depending on the situation

you want to cater for. The most simple is where you decided,
before or soon after the birth, that you want to send your
child to a fee-paying school. A policy can be arranged
which will pay money to meet all or part of the fees, with
or without an inflation hedge, from the year he or she
enters the school. Or, if you have the cash, a scheme can be
set up to invest it in a mixture of *Gilts* and *Insurance*
policies which will mature over the time the child is at
school. It is worth bearing in mind that some schemes rely
on the fact that the money is being sent to a charitable
foundation – the school – so if you decided to go abroad,
or send your child to a state school instead, the money is
locked in. See *Composition fee*, *Independent Schools
Information Service*.

Scrip issue
Officially called a capitalisation issue, this is a distribution
of shares in a company to existing shareholders. They do not
have to pay anything extra, which prompts the illusion that
the shares are free. They're not. They are a recognition
that the company's reserves have grown out of proportion
to its share capital. The reserves are being capitalised. But
the firm's ability to pay dividends is unchanged, so the new
share price often drops after the old shares go 'ex-cap',
which means that any shares you buy will no longer carry a
right to the scrip. However, it is a sign that the company
is in reasonably rude health.

Scripophily
A form of *Alternative investment*. Scripophilists collect
certificates for old companies or busted foreign bonds, not
because they are likely to pay a dividend but because they
are a delight to the eye – and if they delight other eyes
they might rise in value. American railroad stocks are
favourites, as are the ornate Russian and Chinese bonds. With
these, there is always the slight possibility that it might suit
their governments to redeem them.

SEAQ See *Stock Exchange Automated Quotation system*.

Second mortgage
While a first *Mortgage* is normally taken out to help people
to buy a house, the second mortgage is really a way of
using the enhanced value of the house as *Collateral* for a
Loan. If you borrow a 100% mortgage on a £20,000 house, in
10 years' time it may be worth £50,000 or even more. That
gives you £30,000 of *Equity* – if you were to sell, that is
what you would have in your hand after the mortgage was
paid off. If you do not want to move, but want to make
use of that extra value, you can go to a *Building society* or a
Finance house and ask for a second mortgage. They will
probably charge you a higher rate of interest, for their risk
is higher. Some lenders may restrict you to spending the
loan on home improvement. And if you decide to move
house after all, your equity will be that much less.

Securities and Investments Board
The agency expected to carry out the powers vested in the
Secretary of State for the Department of Trade and
Industry under the Financial Services Act. It is also the first
port of call for anyone who has a complaint about an *Investment
business*. Its address is 3 Royal Exchange Buildings, London
EC3V 3NL. Telephone: 01-283 2474.

Self-employed
A self-explanatory term, but those who are self-employed
are across a great tax divide from those who work for other
people. They are deprived of many of the social security and
unemployment safety nets, and have to make their own
arrangements for sickness, pensions and loss of business
while on holiday. However, they pay tax in arrears and
can claim a far wider range of expenses to set against their
tax bill. By the same token, however, the Inland Revenue
can be remarkably suspicious of some of those expenses. It
is worth hiring an accountant to help you through the
maze.

Self-employed pension
This is a type of insurance contract for self-employed people, and those whose firms do not run an *Occupational pension* scheme. As with other insurance policies, the annual premium is limited to less than a sixth of yearly earnings before tax. At retirement age it pays a pension some of which can be taken as a lump sum. There may be tax on the pension itself.

Self-Regulatory Organisation
A group of investment businesses subject to a code of conduct approved by the *Securities and Investments Board*.

Sell
To give up or transfer something, including a person's time, in return for money. Such has been the pressure on salesmen over the years that it has also acquired the more cynical meaning of selling the item that the buyer did not at first want, or getting a high price for it. But if you think you have been sold in this way, the law may help. See *Office of Fair Trading*, *Sale*.

SEPACS See *Sheltered Employment Procurement and Consultancy Services*.

Separate assessment
A husband or wife who is unhappy about having their own financial affairs mixed up with their partner's can ask for separate assessment. In itself, it does not save tax – it merely shares it out differently. It can save rows. It can also start them. Whoever pays the mortgage gets the whole tax relief, and the wife is guaranteed the equivalent of her earned-income allowance. Either spouse can ask for separate assessment without consulting the other.

Separate taxation
If a married couple both work, they may be able to cut their tax bill by opting for separate taxation. Unless you ask to opt,

the husband collects the *Married man's allowance*, the wife
an earned income allowance equal to the *Single person's
allowance*. But their pay is lumped together before the tax
is worked out. This can push them into higher tax rates.
Separate taxation helps them to duck these high bands – but
in return the husband has to go back to the single person's
allowance, which is normally about a third lower. This
trade-off means that separate taxation is worth while only for
a couple earning at least £20,000 together, with the wife
earning at least £7,000 of that. You must make your choice
within six months of the end or the start of the *Fiscal year*.
Take professional advice.

SERPS Stands for State Earnings Related Pensions. See
Earnings Related Pension.

Service potential
The capacity of a business asset to provide a service or make
things. You can work it out in three ways. First, what you
make from selling the asset's output, minus the cost of
running it. Second, the asset's expected useful life. Third,
the number of widgets it makes in a given period. This is
used in *Current cost accounting* to value an asset without
getting muddled by price increases.

Settlement day
On the Stock Exchange, the day when dealing accounts
between *Broker dealers* and *Market makers* have to be
settled.

Settlement discount
This is a discount given to buyers who pay promptly. The
most common example is the cash discount, given for paying
cash immediately the goods are handed over. The normal
credit period is 30 days, and discounts may be allowed for any
buyer who meets this deadline. The discount is a way of
encouraging customers to pay. Some firms add a little to
their standard prices, so that the 'discount' only brings the

price back to where it should be – and the standard price really conceals a penalty for slow payers. See *Discount*, *Trade discount*.

Severance pay
If a trades union is likely to oppose a factory closure, employers sometimes sweeten the pill by offering more than the *Statutory redundancy payment* to the employees to be thrown out of work. This is known as severance pay, and can be used to save time and stop the negotiations dragging on while the factory is losing money.

Sex Discrimination Act See *Equal Pay Act*.

Share
The hard currency of *Limited companies*. When a company is formed it must issue at least two shares. There is no maximum. These shares give the holders the right to decide who the company's directors should be, and through them how the company should be run. They vote on dividend payments to themselves and whether new shares should be created. They are also financially responsible for mishaps, but only to the value of their investment. This is a crucial advantage. Members of *Partnerships*, by contrast, can be stripped of all their personal belongings.

Share certificate
When you buy shares in a company, you are sent a certificate by the company to show how many you own. This is an important document, to be kept in a safe place and sent to your *Broker dealer* when you sell the shares. See *Bearer shares*.

Shareholders' funds
The basic shareholders' fund is the money they have put up in return for the shares they own. British accounting practice is to give shares a par or nominal value – say, 25p, 50p or £1. But in a stock market flotation or a rights issue they

may fetch more than that. Any extra is siphoned into a share premium account. That is also part of shareholders' funds, as are reserves.

Share shop
An office on a street where you can buy and sell shares. Some are owned by members of the Stock Exchange, but they do not have to be. If they boast that they do not charge commission, beware. They are then reckoning to make their profit out of the difference between their buying and selling prices, which may be greater than the comparable difference on the Stock Exchange.

Shekel
Like other ancient currencies, the Israeli shekel was at first a measure of weight – in this case dating back to Babylonian times. It was readopted by Israel when it gained independence in 1948, and its value fluctuates violently.

Shelter
This is a company *limited by guarantee*, which runs what it calls the national campaign for the homeless. It has raised millions of pounds to build housing, and publishes a series of books and pamphlets on the subject. Its address is 157 Waterloo Road, London SE1 8XF.

Sheltered employment
This is the jargon for the *Manpower Services Commission*'s policy of paying local authorities, charities and voluntary bodies to provide work for the disabled under 'sheltered' conditions, by providing special equipment and facilities. It is aimed at those who would not be able to get jobs in 'open' employment. See *Disabled*.

Sheltered Employment Procurement and Consultancy Services
A *Manpower Services Commission* agency which acts as a go-between, seeing to the needs of *Sheltered employment*

workshops from the resources of government purchasing
departments, and thinking up new ways of employing the
disabled. It also gives advice on how to set up sheltered
workshops.

Shilling
Rooted in the Old English word *scilling*, the shilling was
introduced into the national currency by Henry VII as a
coin worth 12 pence. As there were 240 pennies in a pound,
there were automatically 20 shillings in a pound. It is
related to the German Schilling of 1693, now surviving as
the Austrian currency unit. Three former British colonies
– Kenya, Tanzania and Uganda – call their currency the
shilling, as well as the nearby Somali Republic. The Tanzanian
shilling costs 28 to the pound, the Kenyan 24, the Somalian
50 and the Ugandan 2,000.

Short
If you go short of a stock or share, you have promised to
deliver something you have not got, hoping to buy back
later at a lower price. It is also known as going a *Bear*.

Short hedge
A tactic on *Futures* markets whereby a trader *Hedges* by
selling *Futures contracts*.

Shorthold tenancy
This is a tenancy under which the landlord can let a home
at a *Fair rent* for a predetermined period, between one and
five years. Then he will have the right to repossess the
property. See *Assured tenancy*, *Regulated tenancy*, *Tenant*.

Short-time working See *Lay-off*.

SIB See *Securities and Investments Board*.

Sickness benefit
Payable only to people who have paid, or been credited

with, a minimum number of *National Insurance* contributions.
On top of the basic benefit, extra is payable for a wife or
other dependent adult and children, and there is a top-up
related to income. Your first-ever claim must be lodged
within 21 days of the illness beginning, excluding Sundays:
after that, you must claim within six days. A doctor's
statement is needed, but do not wait for it if you are in danger
of being late with your claim. There is a forest of other rules:
your local social security office can give full details. See
Disablement benefit, Injury benefit.

Simple interest
Interest paid on a fixed sum of money. If you lend £100 and
receive £20 plus the original two years later, that is simple
interest of 10%. But see also *Compound interest.*

Single person's allowance
This is the basic personal allowance, and applies to the
unmarried, widowed, divorced, a separated couple if the
husband is not maintaining his wife, and a married couple
who have chosen *Separate taxation.*

Sinking fund
As most assets *Depreciate*, money has to be put aside to buy
replacements. To stop this money from being snapped up
for other projects, it is put into a separate sinking fund.
Such a fund can also be used to repay a loan, or to provide
for the ending of a property lease. The idea was first
introduced to Britain by Sir Robert Walpole in 1716.

Skillcentre
This is a workshop set up under the *Training Opportunities
Scheme*. Each one operates like a small factory, using
up-to-date machinery under the supervision of trained
instructors.

Slump
Originally used to describe stock market collapses, this

evocative word came into its own in the 1930s, when the
world's economies seemed to grind to a halt, causing
widespread poverty and mass unemployment. It is now
reserved as the term for the worst economic state in the
Trade cycle. See also *Boom, Recession*.

Small Business Course
Part of the *Training Opportunities Scheme* run by the
Manpower Services Commission, this is a course designed to
show first-time businessmen the basics of starting their own
ventures. Details can be had from the MSC, Moorfoot,
Sheffield S1 4PQ. See also *Small Firms Service, CoSIRA,
London Enterprise Agency, Business Expansion Scheme*.

Small Claims Court
A slight misnomer. It is not a court, but technically ranks
as a voluntary arbitration scheme. If you are involved in
a dispute over faulty goods or failure to pay for them,
damages, rent arrears or a shortfall on your pay, this is the
place to settle it. Costs are kept to a minimum, as are
formalities. Your local *Citizens' Advice Bureau* can tell you
how to go about it.

Small Firms Service
This is a Department of Trade and Industry service to help
small businesses, and advise people thinking of starting their
own business. It will answer most queries, and it is free for
all but the lengthiest inquiries. There are offices round the
country, but the head office is Small Firms Centre, Ebury
Bridge House, 2–18 Ebury Bridge Road, London SW1W
8QD, or Freefone 2444. See also *Council for Small Industries
in Rural Areas, London Enterprise Agency, New Enterprise
Programme, Small Business Course, Business Expansion
Scheme*.

Smithsonian Agreement
The Smithsonian Institute presides over an imposing mall
of museums and galleries lining the route to the Capitol in

Washington. Here, in 1971, leading countries tried to tidy the tatters of the 1944 *Bretton Woods* system of fixed exchange rates by devaluing the US dollar and agreeing to keep their currencies within 2.25% either side of the new rates. Six months later Britain put the pound into free float.

Social security
The social security system in this country dates from the introduction of *National Insurance* in 1948. It is administered by the Department of Health and Social Security, and attempts to cover just about every type of financial difficulty with at least some money to give people food and shelter. About 80% of the cost comes from *national insurance* contributions, the rest from the government's central funds. Some payments are made to people who have not made contributions, in particular *Supplementary benefit*. Local authorities also give help. The address of your local social security office is in the phone book. The *Citizens' Advice Bureau*, also in the phone book, can give guidance on what and how to claim.

Soft currency
The currency of a country which has been suffering from political or economic problems, making that currency tend to wilt under selling pressure on foreign exchange markets. And the easier it is to hit, the more likely it is that speculators will sell it in the expectation of easy profit. As we have found with the pound, it can be difficult to shed that sort of reputation.

Sole agency
If you are selling a house, a sole agency gives an estate agent the exclusive right to try to sell it. But you are not barred from finding a buyer yourself. However, sole agency is so much the rule now that you should chase your agent up and perhaps even set him a time limit. See *Estate agent*, *Multiple agency*, *Sole selling rights*.

Sole selling rights
This is a rare type of *Estate agent* agreement whereby you give him sole rights to sell your house, and he collects a commission even if you find a buyer yourself. It might be worth it if yours is a particularly undesirable residence. But it hardly gives the agent much of an incentive to get a move on, unless you make it subject to an early deadline. Then you could return to the more normal *Multiple agency*, or *Sole agency*.

Solidus
The middle letter of the £.s.d. monetary system which prevailed in Britain before decimalisation in 1971. Like its two partners, it derives from Latin, in this case a gold coin worth 25 denarii. In England it became worth 12 denarii, or pence. But that was because the *Denarius* had become worth a pennyweight – or a 240th – of a pound. Solidus, through the old, elongated way of writing the letter 's', gradually turned into the '*l*' sign which was used in showing shillings and survives in other ways today.

Solvent
Literally, able to solve or liquidate your obligations. In practice, it means that you are capable of paying your debts. See *Insolvent*.

Son's or daughter's service allowance
If you depend on and maintain a son or daughter who lives with you, and you are infirm or over 64 at the start of the *Fiscal year*, you can claim this tax allowance. It is ruled out if you are already claiming the more valuable *Housekeeper allowance* or *Blind person's allowance*, or if your wife is under 64 and healthy.

Special commissioners
Part of the Inland Revenue, special commissioners are civil servants appointed by the Lord Chancellor who hear appeals by the public against tax assessments. They are

called in only if the taxpayer prefers them to the *General commissioners*. See *Commissioners of Inland Revenue*, *Inland Revenue Tribunal*.

Special deposit
Money which the banks are compelled to lodge with the Bank of England to restrict their ability to lend. Bank lending is limited to a certain multiple of the banks' deposits. The lower those deposits in their own accounts, the less the banks can lend.

Special drawing rights
This is a special form of international currency, used by nation members of the *International Monetary Fund* to help pay their dues and settle debts. They were introduced in 1969 in an attempt to get away from international reliance on gold. Gold, however, persists.

Special grant
This is a type of *Housing grant* issued only in the most needy cases, where there is overcrowding or where the house lacks a bath or lavatory. Like other grants for housing, it is awarded by the local council. See *Improvement grant*, *Repair grant*.

Special hardship allowance
An addition to *Disablement benefit*, for people who cannot return to their original grade of work because of injury or disease. It is an alternative to the *Unemployability supplement*, which is worth more.

Special Temporary Employment Programme
Until 1981, this was the forerunner to the *Community Enterprise Programme*. Unlike its successor, it was confined to assisted areas and was not open to 18-year-olds.

Specie
If you are paid in specie, you get what you ask for. The

phrase's use has shrunk as the precious metal in coins has been diluted with base metals such as lead and zinc. Stemming from the Latin for the actual or specific thing in question, it sprang up in the sixteenth century when Henry VIII began to debase the coinage. If you asked for specie, you were insisting on pure gold or silver. That battle has, however, been lost long ago.

Specific legacy

In a *Will*, a specific *Legacy* is one which stipulates a particular item, such as a block of shares or a set of golf clubs. If the legacy is income-producing, such as stocks or shares, the *Testator* can opt to give the beneficiary any dividends paid between his or her death and the transfer of the gift. To do that, the testator has to waive the Apportionment Act 1870. If that Act applies, then the dividends or interest automatically go into the pot with the rest of the *Estate*.

Speculator

Eternal object of envy and suspicion, the speculator enlivens markets whether he is running against the crowd, or clutching their coat-tails. The word derives from the Latin for a spy or a lookout. Like anyone else, a speculator buys to sell at a higher price, or sells to buy at a lower price. But he is not the sort to wait forever. Beyond a few months, and a speculator becomes an investor: less than a few hours, and a speculator is an out-and-out gambler.

Split-level trust

A type of *Investment trust*. Shares in the trust are divided into income and capital shares. Most or all of the dividends flowing from the trust's investments go to holders of the income shares. When the trust is liquidated, capital gains on the investment portfolio go to the capital shareholders. It is a way of catering efficiently for investors who want a high income, and high taxpayers who already have plenty of income and want future capital gains.

Sporting rights
How sporting it is depends on your point of view, but the right to stalk, shoot or fish can change hands for several thousands of pounds. It can be sold separately from the land on which it takes place, except in Scotland where only salmon fishing can be sold separately. Rates can be charged on the sporting rights alone.

Spot
In *Futures* markets, the spot price is today's price – in contrast to the future price, at which the deal is struck for delivery of the goods in a few months' time. The difference between the two is a measure of what the market thinks is going to happen to the balance between *Supply* and *Demand*. That is why news of a disastrous coffee crop immediately sends the futures price soaring.

Spot month
The next possible *Delivery month* for each type of *Futures contract*.

Spread
On the *Stock Exchange*, the spread or turn is the difference between the buying and selling price of a security. On *Futures* markets, including *Traded options*, it is a tactic whereby a dealer buys and sells two different *Futures contracts* at the same time, hoping that the balance of risk will work in his or her favour. See *Straddle*.

Square mile See *City*.

Squeeze
When an item on a market becomes scarce, anyone who is *Short* of that item has to bid the price up to meet his or her obligations to deliver. If others in the market know the situation, they will squeeze the *Bears* by pushing the price up even more. That is why it is also known as a bear squeeze.

SRO See *Self-Regulatory Organisation.*

Stag
A stock market beast who makes a habit of applying for
shares in companies which are being floated on the market for
the first time. The stags' antlers start twitching if they sense,
through press reports or City gossip, that many more shares
are going to be applied for than are on offer. When this
happens, the shares are handed out by ballot and the price
is likely to jump when market dealings begin a few days
later. To beat the system, stags often send in several
applications under different names to improve their chances
of success in the ballot. If they fail, their cheques are
returned and nothing has been lost. But do not be caught
holding shares in a new issue which no one else wants.

Stagflation
A combination of stagnation and inflation, a phenomenon
which first appeared in modern times during the 1970s.
This period defied the previous accepted wisdom, which
was that a slowing of economic activity will automatically
take the heat out of price rises and wage claims. Some
economists still defend this view, but concede that it now
takes longer to work through. The word 'stagflation' is
believed to have been coined by Sir Patrick Sergeant,
former City Editor of the *Daily Mail.*

Stamp duty
This is a tax which is imposed on the transfer of property,
including stocks and shares. It is collected by the enforced
sale of stamps which must by law be stuck to the documents
relating to the deal in question. It is administered by the
Inland Revenue.

Standing order
This is an instruction to your bank to pay an identical sum
to the same person or company at fixed intervals – monthly,
quarterly, half-yearly or yearly. It is a handy way of paying

easily forgettable bills like mortgage payments or insurance premiums. It can be used for fluctuating bills, like gas or electricity, by agreeing a fixed sum with the recipient and settling the difference at the end of every year. The bank makes a small charge for the service. See also *Direct debit*.

Start-up Scheme See *Business Start-up Scheme*.

State pension
The first State pension appeared in 1908, but dates in its modern form from 1948. All employees then had to contribute to *National Insurance*. It no longer pays for itself, but is used as a 'score board' to decide how much everyone should receive. It now consists of a *Basic component* and an *additional component* reflecting higher salaries. *Earnings related pensions* were introduced by the State in 1961. The first plan was scrapped in 1975, and replaced in 1978 by a system which was due to take full effect in 1998. See *Pension*.

Statutory income
This is the level of income which is taken as the basis for working out a person's tax rate. For most people, it is the income they received in the year before the year in which the tax is actually being deducted. This means that in such cases, tax rates work a year in arrears. This is fine so long as your income is rising, but can be painful if you suffer a pay cut. See also *Taxable income, Total income*.

Statutory Joint Industrial Council
This is very similar to a *Wages Council*, except that it does not include any independent members. It is made up solely of representatives of employers and employees, and has power to determine minimum pay and conditions for a particular industry. It must be set up by the Secretary of State for Employment, after consulting the *Advisory, Conciliation and Arbitration Service*.

Statutory redundancy payment
There is a complex set of rules to decide how much an

employee is entitled to if he or she is *Redundant*. Essentially,
it is a lump sum worked out on the basis of *Length of
service*: 1½ weeks' pay for every year served between the ages
41 to 65, 1 week for every year when the employee was
between 22 and 41, and half a week for every year between
18 and 22. But this is the minimum. Some trade unions
have negotiated better terms. The employer has to show
how each individual's payment was arrived at, and this can be
checked against the rules set out in a Department of
Employment booklet, *The Redundancy Payments Scheme*. See
also *Retention pay*, *Severance
pay*.

Stockbroker
The name for a *Broker dealer* on the Stock Exchange before
the change to *Dual capacity* in October 1986.

Stock Exchange
Any market for the exchange of securities is a stock
exchange, and every major western country has at least
one. The biggest are in New York, Tokyo and London. The
London exchange is in fact part of a national network,
based in the City but linked to several provincial centres. In
turn, many provincial stockbrokers have offices in
London. See *Unlisted Securities Market*.

Stock Exchange Automated Quotation System
This is the electronic price display system which is central
to the new Stock Exchange structure. All market makers must
register their bid and offer prices with the system, along
with the maximum size in which they are prepared to deal.

Stock Exchange Daily Office List
This is a list of all *Quoted securities*, giving their latest
dividend, *Ex-dividend* date and date of payment, the official
price at 2.15 p.m. that day and the prices at which *Bargains*
have been *Marked*. The *Official List*, which can be obtained
from the *Stock Exchange*, is taken as the yardstick for most

legal valuations of shares. Paradoxically, it also includes the prices of shares on the *Unlisted securities market*.

Stockjobber
A jobber stands on the floor of the stock exchange, ready to deal with brokers who come to carry out the instructions of their clients. A jobber trades shares for himself. He quotes two prices for a share: he will buy from the broker at the lower price and sell to him at the higher. The difference is known as the jobber's turn and is his main source of income. A jobber can of course also make profits on the shares he holds or goes short of. This function is due to be abolished in its traditional form in 1986. See *Market maker*, *Primary dealer*.

Stock turnover
A good measure of the efficiency of a company is to see how quickly it shifts its stocks. The longer they lie idle, the more money is being tied up unnecessarily. In some businesses, like heavy engineering, this cannot be helped. Shops, on the other hand, should keep stocks on the move all the time. Stock turnover can be worked out from a *Balance sheet* by dividing the stocks figure into the annual *Turnover*.

Stop-loss
A Stock Exchange term for a standing order given by an investor to a stockbroker to buy or sell within specified prices. It is an attempt to put a selling floor under a falling price, or a buying ceiling on a rising price.

Stop order See *Limit order*.

Straddle
A tactic on *Futures* or *Traded options* markets. The idea is to buy and sell at the same time contracts in the same underlying *Security* or *Commodity*, for *Delivery* in different months. It is a type of *Spread*.

Straight line method

The simplest way to work out the *Depreciation* on an asset.
You take the asset's cost, guess when it will need replacing
and what its scrap value will be then. Subtract the scrap
value from the cost price, and divide that by the number
of years you plan to use it. The result will be the amount of
depreciation per year. This method does not take account
of repair charges. See *Diminishing balance method*,
Revaluation method.

Subscription share account

One of the range of building society savings accounts. This
one pays extra interest on condition that you deposit an
agreed sum every month. As such, it is also a very good way
of showing the society that you are capable of keeping up
Mortgage payments. See *Building society*, *Escalator share*,
Ordinary share account, *Term share*.

Subsidiary

A subsidiary company is one that is controlled by another
company. Large companies often have many subsidiaries
to handle different trading operations.

Subsidy

A subsidy is a grant or financial aid. But, down the ages, it
has been a moot point as to who was supposed to be
helping whom. A feudal prince used to exact a subsidy from
the peasantry to help him with special expense such as war
or building work. Since 1867, however, it has settled down
as the word for government aid to a public authority or
nationalised industry. There are also subsidy schemes to
help people buy or improve their homes.

Subsistence

Subsistence is the ability to have an independent existence.
In money terms, it refers to the minimum income needed to
achieve that state. See *Subsistence theory of wages*.

Subsistence theory of wages
Part of *Classical economics*, this theory claimed that if
workers were paid any more than a *Subsistence* wage level, the
population would increase. This assumed that any extra
money would be devoted solely to having and rearing children.
The theory appeared to be true for the half-century either
side of 1800, but in richer economies pay rises are just as
likely to be spent on buying a better standard of living.

Succession tax See *Inheritance Tax*.

Sucre
One of the most colourfully-named currencies in the world,
this Ecuadorian unit is not, as might seem, named after the
French word for sugar. It is a tribute to Antonio Jose de
Sucre, a leading figure in Ecuador, and became the
money's title in 1886. There are two rates for the sucre: the
'official' at 160 to the pound, and the 'free' at about 190.

Sunspot theory
An economist called Jevons (1835–1882) noticed a link
between the *Trade cycle* and changes in the amount of
sunspots – dark patches on the surface of the sun. It sounds
far-fetched, but the thread of logic comes through the
influence of sunspots on weather and therefore harvests. It
may be growing less important as food takes a smaller and
smaller slice of our income.

Superannuation fund
Superannuation is a word for being over-age, and a
superannuation fund is a fund for such people – to pay
their *Pension*. Apart from the *State pension*, most companies
provide an *Occupational pension*, and this is what a
superannuation fund usually refers to.

Superannuation Funds Office
This is a branch of the *Inland Revenue*, set up to vet
Occupational pension schemes to make sure that they are

eligible for tax privileges. It has developed a code of practice
which lays out the criteria for approval. The SFO is at
Lynwood Road, Thames Ditton, Surrey KTY 0DP, where
it works closely with the *Occupational Pensions Board*.

Supplementary benefit

This is a *Means-tested* benefit for people who are not in
full-time work, and do not have enough to live on. You have
to show that you are poor by revealing how much savings
you have. Women cannot claim it if they are married or
living with a man as a common-law wife. Unlike
Unemployment benefit, you do not have to have paid National
Insurance contributions. Full details are available in leaflet
SB.1, from social security offices.

Supplementary pension

This is a means-tested addition to the *State pension*. You
must apply to your local office of the Department of Health
and Social Security – under Health in the phone book – who
will decide how much money you need, and set that against
details you must tell them regarding your income and
savings. Do not be put off by all that if you are finding it hard
to make ends meet.

Supply

Supply is an economic concept based on the idea that the
higher the price of an article, the higher the potential profit
for manufacturers and so the more they will produce. In
that sense, it is the converse of *Demand* by consumers.
The theory is that the *Price* will be fixed at the point where
supply and demand are matched. See *Economics*, *Elasticity*,
Macro-economics, *Micro-economics*.

Supply of Goods and Services Act

Passed in 1982, this Act extends the principles of the *Sale
of Goods Act* to services and to goods which are supplied in
ways other than by sale. This can take in goods hired,
bartered or supplied through a repair, like car parts. The

goods have to be fit, useful for the intended purpose and in
reasonable condition. Services have to be performed with
reasonable care and at reasonable cost. 'Reasonable' is
ultimately defined by the courts. See *Consumer law*.

Supply of Goods (Implied Terms) Act
This 1973 Act closed some of the loopholes which
shopkeepers had spotted in the *Sale of Goods Act*.
Guarantees can no longer take your rights away: they can
only extend your rights by giving you some chance to
tackle the manufacturer as well as the retailer. You can
cancel your contract if the goods are faulty, or keep the
goods and claim damages. This makes nonsense of the
now-illegal shop-window assertion, 'no refunds given'.

Surrender
Something to avoid on the *Insurance* battlefield. You are
legally entitled to surrender an insurance policy up to 10 days
after signing for it. After that, you will be charged heavily
for cashing in earlier than the policy's agreed term. In the
first two years you may get nothing: from then on, a notional
interest rate, minus the insurer's costs. Some Canadian
insurers offer guaranteed cash-in values, but these are paid
for by giving a lower return to those who stay the course.
If you are hard up, discuss it with either the insurance firm
or your broker. Two steps better than surrender are, first, to
stop paying the premiums – you can always restart later –
or, if you have had the policy for at least three years, to
ask your bank to take it as *Collateral* on an *Overdraft*.

Surveyors
Most people will come across surveyors only when they are
buying a house. Nowadays, building societies will
sometimes let you read the survey they commission to verify
that the house merits the value of the mortgage you are
asking for. But you may have to order your own. It will read
like a horror story, because surveyors tend to point out
every little crack to prevent any comebacks later. The

important thing is to make sure that they have looked at all
the main areas – walls, floors, ceilings, roof, doors, windows
and outhouses, as well as the water, electrical and heating
systems. If you are genuinely worried by the surveyor's
criticisms, consult your solicitor. See *Incorporated Society
of Valuers and Auctioneers* and *Royal Institution of Chartered
Surveyors*.

Suspense account
If a *Bookkeeper's Trial balance* does not balance, he has to
comb the books for the mistake. Sometimes it cannot be
found, or a firm may decide that it is not worth the time
and trouble to search. The temporary answer is to put the
missing sum into a suspense account, which is really a
collection of such errors. Eventually they should be picked
up, particularly if creditors have not been paid as a result.

Switching
Moving from one investment to another in one manoeuvre,
by selling the first and buying the second. To be truly
considered switching, the two types of investment must be
related, such as two *Gilts*, or chemical shares, or
currencies.

Taka
The currency of Bangladesh, the country which emerged
out of a revolution in the former East Pakistan in 1971.
There are 45 taka to the pound, and they are divided into
100 poisha. Taka come in notes of 1, 5, 10, 50, 100 and
500.

Takeover
A takeover happens when one individual or company buys
all the shares in another company by bidding the same price
to all the shareholders. The bidder can offer cash, his own
shares or a variety of loan stock. Normally the takeover
will not go through unless more than half the shares are
pledged to the bidder. If he collects over 90% of the shares,

the bidder can apply through the courts to acquire the rest
compulsorily. See *Merger, Takeover panel*.

Takeover Panel
A body originally set up under the wing of the *Council for
the Securities Industry* to see fair play in takeovers or mergers
involving companies whose shares are quoted on the British
stock market. It does not have the force of law, but it
publishes a code of rules. If it sees wrongdoing it can censure
the culprit or even order share dealings to be unwound.
The guilty can ignore the Panel's rulings, but the penalty
may be that no stockbroker or bank will act for them.
Beyond that, the courts or the Department of Trade and
Industry have to step in. See also *Securities and Investment
Board*.

Tala
The currency unit of Western Samoa in the Pacific. The tala
is worth 30p.

Talisman
This is the acronym for the system used to settle *Bargains*
on the *Stock Exchange*. It stands for Transfer Accounting,
Lodgement for Investors, Stock MANagement for jobbers.
All the *Securities* sold during a day are transferred to a special
company, Stock Exchange Pool Nominees, or SEPON, and
there are separate accounts for each *Market maker*. From there
the stock is passed to the *Broker dealer* acting for the buyer,
and the cash value goes to the selling broker.

Tap
This is an issue of securities, nowadays almost always from
the government, which is floated on to the market in dribs
and drabs. There are two reasons: one is that issues of
government stock are often too large for the stock market
to absorb in one go, without bringing prices crashing down.
The other reason is that the tap enables the government
to influence interest rates through the amount and price of

the stock floated at any given time. Some stock, such as *Treasury bills*, are usually sold by *Tender*.

Tariff
In a restaurant or pub, a tariff is a list of prices. In international trade, a tariff is a tax imposed on imports by the importing country. It is usually worked out as a percentage of the price at which the goods land at the docks. The idea behind it is to hold down the level of imports of the goods in question.

Tax
Compulsory payment to the government under laws laid down by successive Finance Acts designed to produce government revenue according to the political principles in force at the time. That is the formal definition behind the ritual of the Chancellor of the Exchequer's annual *Budget*. In practice, we tend to think of the individual taxes and their broad types: *Direct, Indirect, Progressive, Regressive, Capital tax, Income tax, Customs duty, Excise duty, Value-Added Tax, Profits tax, Death duty, Estate duty, Capital Gains Tax, Inheritance Tax, Payroll tax, Poll tax, Capitation tax, Property tax, Rates, Purchase tax, Sales tax, Stamp duty, Surtax, Corporation tax, Imputation tax*. Happily, we do not suffer all of these. See also *Allowances, Tax relief* and *Deductible expenses*.

Tax and Prices Index
This was introduced by Sir Geoffrey Howe, the then Chancellor of the Exchequer, in 1979. He argued that the *Retail Prices Index* was being unfairly distorted by indirect taxes like VAT and did not allow for the cuts in income tax which he was proposing at that time. But custom and usage have kept the RPI to the fore.

Tax code
A vital part of the *Pay As You Earn* tax-collecting system. So that your employer knows how much of your pay to

withhold for tax, the Inland Revenue gives the firm a code, consisting of three figures and a letter. You are given the same information in a *Notice of Coding*. The three figures show your total allowances, minus the last figure. If your allowances are £3,456, the code will show 345. The letter shows your tax status: L for a single person or working wife, H for a married man, T a single pensioner, V a married pensioner, F a pensioner on a higher rate of tax, D for a non-pensioner on higher tax, BR for a taxpayer on basic rate but with a second job. O is basic rate, NT means no tax. An employee can object to his employer knowing his personal situation, in which case L is used. Without a proper code, you are automatically given an emergency coding, which is more severe – though the extra tax is refundable later. See *P45*, *P60*, *Tax deduction card*.

Tax deduction card
After a *Notice of Coding* has been sent to an employee, the employer receives a tax deduction card. This shows the employee's tax code, and authorises the employer to deduct tax from the employee's pay.

Tax deduction certificate
If you are the *Beneficiary* of a *Will*, you should make sure that the *Executor* sends you one of these certificates if there is any chance of having to pay *Income tax*. This is unlikely to matter if you simply receive a cash sum or an heirloom. But if the will sets up a *Trust*, you will need a certificate so that you can fill in your own tax return properly.

Tax haven
A tax haven is anywhere you can live or invest so as to pay less tax. Britain is one of the most popular havens with foreigners. This is because a major consideration is that the haven should be politically stable: saving tax is futile if you or your money end up on the point of a bayonet. The Channel Islands and the Isle of Man are attractive, as they are British run and nearby. Others are in the Caribbean or

odd pockets of Europe such as Liechtenstein,
Luxembourg or Andorra. All have snags, though, so look
carefully before you leap. See *Non-resident*, *Offshore fund*.

Tax relief
A tax relief is any spending which you are allowed to deduct
from income or profits before the tax is worked out. In Britain
such reliefs are sometimes called allowances if they are a
fixed cash sum, like *Personal allowances*. See *Tax*.

Tax year See *Fiscal year*.

Taxable income
This is a person's *Total income*, minus *Personal allowances*.

Technical analysis See *Charts*.

Tenant
Coming from the Latin *tenere*, to hold, a tenant was originally
anyone who held land. It became whittled down to people
who do not own land, but have the right to occupy it for a
fixed period. The state of being a tenant is called tenantry.
Over the years, there has been a sheaf of laws designed to
produce a fair deal between tenants and landlords. See
*Fair rent, Federation of Private Residents' Associations, Rent
allowance, Rent rebate*.

Tender
An aggressive way to float a company's shares on the stock
market – effectively by auction. The issuing house strikes a
price, to give would-be investors an idea of what to go for.
The public then applies to buy the number of shares they
each want, at a price of their own choice. When all the bids
are in, the price is taken which will clear all the shares.
To succeed, a tender needs a rush of buyers, and often stems
from a fear that an *Offer for sale* by a fixed price will give
the *Stags* too much profit. But a tender can be an unholy
flop.

Term insurance
The purest form of life insurance. It pays a fixed sum if
death occurs by a certain date. The money is not invested,
at least not to the policyholder's benefit. It is a straight bet
based on the likelihood of the named person dying, given
his or her age and health at the outset. No death, no payout.
Its virtue is that term insurance gives big cover for the
smallest premium, so is attractive for young breadwinners.
See *Life insurance*, *Whole life insurance*.

Term shares
This is a type of building society saving, where the saver
deposits a lump sum for an agreed minimum period. In return,
the society pays a higher rate of interest. The exact deal
varies from society to society, so it is worth shopping
around. See *Building society*, *Escalator share*, *Ordinary share
account*, *Subscription share account*.

Terminal loss
This is a loss which can occur when a business is closed. It
can be offset against the previous three years' tax bill, so
long as it is not counted twice under some other tax
provision.

Terms of trade
An economist's way of analysing the relationship between
the prices of a country's exports and imports. If import prices
drop while export prices rise, then the terms of trade have
improved. On the other hand, if the export customers are
quick to react to a rise in those prices, the volume of exports
may itself fall: result, unhappiness.

Testator
Someone who makes a *Will*. The word comes from the Latin
testari, meaning to bear witness. If you do not make a will,
you are *Intestate*.

Third-party insurance See *Motor insurance*.

Thirty-share Index See *FT Index*.

Three-column cash book
This is a vital tool in the bookkeeper's art. It is important
to keep a firm's cash and cheque records apart. But it
would be tiresome for a cashier to have to enter them into
separate books, because of the constant need to switch
from one to the other. So the two are cleverly combined on
the same page, using the three-column system. On both
the debtor and creditor sides of the page are columns for the
bank account, cash account, and discounts given or taken.
There is also room for the date, details of each *Transaction*
and the *Folio number*.

Three I's See *Investors In Industry*.

Tick See *Basis point*.

Time deposit See *Deposit account*.

Times covered See *Dividend cover*.

Token money See *Coin, Banknote*.

TOPS See *Training Opportunities Scheme*.

Total income
For tax purposes, total income is someone's *Statutory income*
(and his wife's), less such charges as interest payments. Total
income is used for calculating some tax allowances. See
Taxable income.

Trade
The humble business of selling goods or services, much
derided by the Victorians who were ashamed of the thought
of being 'in trade'. It has developed two distinct nuances.

One is that of the trader, synonymous with a merchant, who lives by buying and selling, taking a profit from the difference. The other is that of the craftsman who learns a trade which he then sells to whoever wants it at the best price he can get. See also *Profession*.

Trade cycle

This is an economists' term to sum up the differing levels of activity as an economy moves from *Boom* to *Slump* and back again. Much effort has been spent on trying to find out exactly why and how these shifts take place. All in vain, beyond the mundane conclusion that they reflect the collective changes in people's mood in response to random events. See also *Depression, Recession*.

Trade and Industry, Department of

The government department responsible for *Consumer laws*, including those designed to protect the public from fraudulent investment schemes and advice. Its address is 1 Victoria Street, London SW1H 0ET.

Trade Descriptions Act

A weakness of the *Misrepresentation Act* is that traders can wriggle out of it if they can claim they did not intend to mislead. That is no excuse here – and the Act also applies when a trader buys from you. He must not con you with a claim that your goods are worse than they are. If you think you have a case, you should go to the *Trading Standards Department* at your local town hall.

Trade discount

This is the difference between what a shopkeeper pays for goods and what he sells them at. It is a discount on the *Recommended retail price*, to give the retailer his *Profit margin*. On many goods the retailer can charge less than the maker's recommended price if he thinks it worth giving up some profit margin to sell the goods more quickly.

Traded options
These are a recent development on the London stock
market. A range of shares is listed, and you can trade in
the right to buy or sell those shares at a fixed price during
a three-month period. For a speculator, the effect is that he
can buy an option on a large block of shares for only a few
hundred pounds. If the shares go down, the option may
be worthless. But if they go up, the profit can flow straight
through to the option price, which the speculator can then
sell. He does not have to take up the option so long as
someone else is willing to buy it. Large institutional
shareholders can 'write' or offer options on part of their
huge portfolios of shares, which they would not otherwise
want to trade on the full stock market.

Trading account
Once a bookkeeper or accountant has done a successful *Trial
balance*, he can go on to analyse it to produce the *Final
account*. The first step is to produce a trading account, which
shows whether the firm is making a profit or loss on sheer
trading: sales minus cost of sales. This gives the gross profit.
Next comes the finished profit-and-loss account, which
shows the *Net profit*.

Trading Standards Department
Part of your local authority, responsible for enforcing
Consumer law. This department should be your first stop
if you have a consumer grievance, but it will also liaise
closely with the *Office of Fair Trading*.

Training for Skills Programme
This is a *Manpower Services Commission* programme under
which the government gives money for the MSC to support a
number of apprentice places each year, complemented by
the *Training Opportunities Scheme*.

Training Opportunities Scheme
This is a government scheme run by the *Training Services*

Division of the *Manpower Services Commission*. If you are
over 19 and have been out of full-time education for two
years or more you can apply to go on one of about 500
courses covering most industries and office skills, including
business administration. You are paid, and can get some
expenses. Ask at your local *Job Centre* for details. See also
New Enterprise Programme, Small Business Course.

Training Services Division
The part of the *Manpower Services Commission* responsible
for devising training schemes, both for individual industries
and to help the unemployed find jobs. There are several
industry training boards, and the division runs the *Training
Opportunities Scheme*, the *Training for Skills Programme* and
Direct Training Services, and puts money into two young
people's schemes, *Community Industry* and *Unified Vocational
Preparation*. See also *Industrial Language Training Service,
Youth Training Scheme*.

Transaction
Transactions are the building blocks of a business. A
transaction is the moment when the customer buys an
article or a service in exchange for money. In a cash
transaction, the money is handed over immediately, but
in credit transactions it follows later.

Travel & Entertainment Cards
Often known as T & Es, these are the posher cousins of the
humble *Credit card*. The main examples in Britain are
American Express and Diners Club. The difference is that
T & Es do not stoop so low as to offer credit. You can use
them to buy things – at a more exclusive and expensive list
of shops than with credit cards – but you are expected to
pay off the whole bill at the end of each monthly period.
While the credit card firms spend millions on advertising
to encourage their cardholders to stay in debt, the T & E
people will send you a sharp reminder to pay up. Another
main difference is that the T & Es charge you a signing-on

fee and an annual subscription. But they can be handier
for businessmen who do a lot of travel and want to impress
their lunch guests.

Travel insurance
It is obviously easier to lose things when you are on a long
journey, and accidents can be more expensive if you are in a
foreign country because of different legal systems. Travel
insurance is usually sold in a package to cover the most
frequent problems. These are lost or damaged property,
personal injury or illness, and the risk of having to cancel the
trip at the last minute. Motorists should also take out extra
cover if they are going abroad. Medical protection is the
most important point. You should check how much a
hospital bed could cost in the country you are visiting.
The US can be notoriously dear, and cover of at least £50,000
is advisable. European Community countries have a
mutual scheme: ask your travel agent or social security
office.

Travellers' cheque
This is a useful means of carrying money around when you
are travelling away from home, especially abroad. All banks
either issue them or can get them for you, as do American
Express and Thomas Cook. You can have them
denominated in any major currency, though if you are
visiting several countries on one trip the most widely accepted
nowadays is the US dollar. They come in a chequebook-style
wallet, usually in several denominations from the
equivalent of £5 to £100. Your security is that you sign each
one when you receive them. Then you sign again when
you want to cash one and the shop or bank can see that the
signatures match. And if they are stolen you will be
automatically repaid by the issuer, but some take longer
than others to cough up.

Treasury
The UK government department responsible for overall

economic policy. It oversees the government's spending
and the taxes and borrowing needed to finance it, the
exchange rate, and the development of longer-term
economic forecasts and plans. In other countries the
equivalent department is often called the Ministry of Finance.

Treasury bills
First suggested by Walter Bagehot, the constitutional
expert, as a means for the government to raise short-term
Finance in the 1870s, Treasury Bills have become a major
instrument of economic policy. Some Treasury Bills are
issued on *Tap* to government departments, but the bulk are
sold to the public at a *Tender* every Friday. Bidders offer
different levels of discount, but they do not know what other
bidders are offering, nor how much the *Treasury* wants to
sell that week. But – and this is a highly professional business
– they do know the state of the *Money market* and the trend
of interest rates. The lowest discount get the bills. The
bidders are London Discount houses and overseas
institutions. Because the government is such a heavy
borrower, it can shift interest rates up or down by flooding
the market with Treasury Bills or keeping them scarce: the
City soon takes the hint. Like other *Bills of exchange*, the
Treasury's normally last three months and are traded on the
Discount market.

Trial balance
This is the accountant's attempt to make his books balance.
If they do not, there must be a mistake in his *Double-entry
Bookkeeping* system, and he has to track it down. If they do,
he can go on to the *Final account*.

Trillion
Like *Billion*, the British trillion has suffered from an
American takeover. A trillion in the US is a million million
or a thousand billion. As most currencies are in smaller units
than the pound, many countries like Japan are already
used to the US trillion and we are likely to go the same way.

The fading British trillion is equal to a million times a
million times a million.

True rate
When you repay a loan in instalments, there are two main
ways of calculating the interest rate. The so-called true rate
points to the fact that you have the money for less time than
many people imagine. If you borrow £100 and repay it in
equal instalments over a year, your average loan has really
been only about £50. So if the lender puts an interest rate
of 10% on the £100, the true rate works out at just under
20%. See *Annual percentage rate*, *Flat rate*.

Trust
A trust is a legal agreement for one group of people to
manage an asset for another group of people. It can be
imposed by someone else, as when money left in a will is
put in trust until the inheritors – particularly children –
meet certain conditions, such as reaching a certain age or
marrying a Nobel Prize winner. Trusts can be voluntary,
like *Unit trusts* or *Investment trusts*. In the US, a trust refers
to groups of companies trying to achieve a *Monopoly*. There
is a series of anti-trust laws to prevent this.

Trustee
Someone who is trusted to manage a *Trust*.

Tugrik
The Ulan Bator Hotel in Mongolia will give you about five
tugriks in exchange for a pound. Import and export of the
tugrik is strictly forbidden.

Turn See *Spread*.

Turnover
The accountants' word for sales. To them, it is the amount
of stock a business turns over. Americans think us quaint for
using such a term: in the US sales are income, and that's

THREE NIGHTS, THAT'S A TRILLION TUGRIKS
GRAND HOTEL ULAN BATOR
NICK BAKER

that. But turnover does point to a useful way of spotting
how efficient a firm is. If you divide the turnover by the
stock in the balance sheet, the higher the result the better.
It is best judged by comparing similar companies, or
scanning the trend of one firm over several years.

Undercapitalised
If a firm is undercapitalised, it is probably *Overtrading*. The
money behind the firm is not enough to handle the amount
of business it is taking on, and its directors may be borrowing
more than is wise. See *Overcapitalised*.

Underinsurance
If you insure the contents of your house for £5,000 when
they are really worth £10,000, you are underinsured. In return
for paying only half the premium you should, if any item is
damaged or stolen you will be paid only half its value by
the insurer. Underinsurance can happen easily when prices
are rising. It is a frustrating fact of life that overinsurance
is just as useless. To punish fraud, the insurer will still pay
only the true value of the goods lost. See *Loss adjuster*,
Loss assessor.

Underwriter
An underwriter literally writes his name under a legal
document, usually an insurance policy or company share issue,
to show that he will guarantee it. The underwriter in effect
says that, under certain conditions, he will pay the agreed
amount of money. The conditions of an insurance policy are
that the event being insured against actually happens. At
Lloyd's insurance market in London, the risk is split among
20 or more underwriters acting for syndicates.

Unearned income
This is a now-obsolete term for income from investments
and property – as opposed to income from the sweat of
the brow or the push of the pen, which was reckoned to be
earned. The distinction was used as a basis for taxing

unearned income more harshly, in the form of the investment income surcharge until 1984.

Unemployability supplement
Paid to people receiving *Disablement benefit*, but who are likely to be permanently unable to work because of their disability. It is worth more than the *Special hardship allowance*, but only one of the two can be claimed at one time.

Unemployment
If you are out of a job, you are unemployed. Unemployment is the condition of being jobless, or the number out of work in a region or country. Economists have identified several causes of unemployment, but no one has yet come up with a foolproof way of controlling it. Some unemployment is temporary, to do with seasonal changes or the weather. Some may be caused by people being unwilling to move to where jobs are vacant. A few people are unable to work because of age or disability. But the biggest cause in the 1970s and 1980s was a worldwide recession combined with big changes in the structure of industry.

Unemployment benefit
For a year after being thrown out of work, the jobless are entitled to a weekly payment through the local *Social Security* office. It is strictly a benefit paid under the *National Insurance* scheme, and to get it you have to have paid National Insurance contributions. If you have not done so, you must apply for *Supplementary benefit*.

Unfair Contract Terms Act
This Act stops traders from padding contracts with get-out clauses. They are specifically banned from disclaiming liability for death or personal injury, and other exclusions must be reasonable. So do not be put off by restaurants stating that they accept no responsibility for loss or damage to diners' property. If the owner's dog chews a sleeve off your coat, you can still prosecute. See *Consumer law*.

Unfair dismissal
Under the Employment Protection Act, a *Dismissal* must
fall into one of four types to be considered fair. It must
be *redundancy*, it must not be biased against trades union
members, it must be based on an agreed selection system, and
it must not discriminate on grounds of sex, race or marital
status. And the employer must show that he has done all
he can to avoid redundancies. But employees have to have
been working for the firm for a year before they can sue
for unfair dismissal.

Unfranked income See *Franked income*.

Unified Vocational Preparation
This is a *Manpower Services Commission* scheme offering
money to firms willing to give school leavers a course including
initial training, work experience and further education.

Unit trust
A fund of money invested on behalf of the public, who are
given units in proportion to the amount they pay in. The
price of the units goes up and down with the value of the
underlying investments – usually shares or gilts, but
property is popular. New units can be issued as more
investors come into the pool. The trusts are run by
management companies, who make an initial charge and
take an annual fee. The Department of Trade is legally
responsible for policing unit trusts. Most belong to the Unit
Trust Association, 16 Finsbury Circus, London EC2M
7JP.

United Nations
The UN was set up by a charter signed at San Francisco in
1945. It is a forum for discussing international political
issues, which mainly lie outside the scope of this book.
However, it has important economic and financial
agencies. It has its own economic and social council, and
economic commissions for the major continents. Also

affiliated to the UN are the *International Monetary Fund* and
World Bank. The UN London Information Centre is at
14–15 Stratford Place W1N 9AF.

Unitisation
An ugly word to describe the process of turning an *Investment
trust* into a *Unit trust*. This is done because shares in investment
trusts often change hands on the Stock Exchange at far less
than the value of the trust's investment portfolio. Unit
trust units, on the other hand, are automatically priced to
reflect the value of the portfolio.

Unit-linked insurance
This is a variation on the with-profits insurance theme. After
administrative costs have been met, the premiums are invested
in a *Unit trust*, which in turn may buy shares, government
stock, property or a mixture of all three. Some unit-linked
schemes guarantee to repay at least your premiums at the
end: otherwise, your fortunes will fluctuate with the value
of the underlying units. Because your last premium may
coincide with a time when the stock market is on its back,
make sure your policy gives you the right to hold on until
you want to cash in. Although the value of the units will
tend to rise, this form of insurance is not for first-time
insurance customers. Get something more basic first.

Unlimited company
This is a way of issuing shares in a business without suffering
all the restrictions of forming a *Limited company*. An
unlimited company can buy back its own shares without
difficulty, and does not have to file accounts with the
Registrar of Companies. But if the company is liquidated,
shareholders and those who held shares in the previous year
may personally have to meet any debts not covered by the
company's assets. See also *Partnership*, *Limited by
guarantee*.

Unlisted Securities Market
This is part of the *Stock Exchange*. It was started in 1980 so

that smaller companies could obtain a *Share quote* without having to go through all the expense of a full *Quotation*. In effect, the Stock Exchange is warning investors that shares on the USM are more risky. See *Over-the-counter market*.

Unsafe goods See *Consumer Protection Act*.

Unsolicited Goods and Services Act
Traders cannot dump goods on you – or do a service like window-cleaning – without your say-so, and then expect you to pay. Threatening letters demanding payment are illegal, and will be pursued by your local *Trading Standards Department*. With unwanted goods, you can either keep them safely for six months, after which they become yours, or you can tell the seller where to collect them – in which case he or she has 30 days to pick them up. See *Consumer law*.

Upper earnings limit
National Insurance contributions are worked out as a percentage of your weekly income, up to a ceiling level. Everyone earning more than the ceiling figure still pays no more than if they were at the ceiling. The limit is currently £220, but it is frequently adjusted.

USM See *Unlisted Securities Market*.

Usury
This word originally referred to any moneylending at a rate of interest, but it became narrowed down to lending at very high interest rates. There is no legal ceiling on interest rates in Britain. Each case is decided on its merits by the courts, but lenders must tell you their *True rate* beforehand.

Value
The worth of something. It is usually measured in money, but any yardstick will do, whether it is a bag of pebbles on your right arm or a straight barter.

Value-Added Tax
Next to parking fees, one of the most disliked taxes. VAT
is charged on all but a small list of goods and services
supplied or imported into the United Kingdom. It was
introduced on 1 April 1973. The tax is levied at each stage of
production and passed on down the line until it reaches the
consumer, who has no one to pass it on to. This means
that businesses have to spend a lot of time keeping track of
their VAT payments and receipts, which are divided into
the input tax and the output tax. The tax has to be logged
by every registered trader, and it is supervised by the
Customs and Excise Department. See also *Exempt, Zero-rating*.

Variable costs See *Direct expenses*.

Variation margin
This is the daily gain or loss on *Open contracts* in a *Futures*
market. At the end of the day it is credited or debited to the
members' accounts, and by them to their clients. See *Eligible
margin, Initial margin, Maintenance margin, Margin call*.

VAT See *Value-Added Tax*.

Vatu
The currency of Vanuatu in the Fiji Islands east of Australia,
it costs 140 to the pound. Vanuatu also accepts the Australian
dollar.

Venture
Carrying the same notion of danger and risk about it, venture
seems like a more hesitant version of *Enterprise*. In recent
years it has tended to refer to young *Businesses*, and a minor
financial industry has sprung up to provide *Venture capital* for
infant companies.

Venture capital
Stung by criticism that it invests only in sure-fire winners,
the City has hesitantly given birth to a series of financial

concerns devoted to offering to lend money to or buy shares in fledgling companies. This money is called venture capital, and normally involves the finance house taking a large *Equity* stake, possibly over 50%, to keep an eye on any loan it has made. This can be galling to the man who has built a small business from nothing, but it can also be an unavoidable step to the big time. See *Venture, Industrial and Commercial Finance Corporation.*

Visible exports/imports See *Current account.*

Wage
The older English word for the money paid to employees. It has gradually come to mean specifically the weekly payment to blue-collar workers. See *Salary.*

Wages book
As wage payment has become more complicated over the years, so the *Bookkeeper*'s wages book has had to follow suit. A typical entry will have a reference number for the employee, his or her name, basic pay, overtime, other payments, gross pay, tax, National Insurance, pension contribution, voluntary deductions, net pay, refunds or advances, and total payable. Then there will be a separate section showing the totals for the *Tax year* so far. See *Wages system.*

Wages Council
This is a body, working under the Wages Act 1986, which sets minimum pay for an industry which has no existing bargaining system. It tends to cover small, fragmented trades such as laundries, millinery, waste reclamation and the exotically named Ostrich and Fancy Feather and Artificial Flower Wages Council. Each one includes representatives of workers and management, and three independent members. The councils are set up by the Secretary of State for Employment, who can also abolish them. They are administered by the Office of Wages Councils, 11 Tothill

Street, London SW1 9NF. See also *Statutory Joint Industrial Council, Wages Inspector*.

Wages Inspector
A person appointed by the Secretary of State for Employment, to ensure that firms are complying with the minimum pay laid down by their *Wages Council*, if there is one. Offenders can be taken to court, and may have to pay arrears of wages. The London office of the wages inspectorate is at Hanway House, Red Lion Square, London, WC1R 4ND. There are also offices at Birmingham, Brighton, Bristol, Cardiff, Edinburgh, Glasgow, Hemel Hempstead, Ipswich, Leeds, Manchester, Newcastle upon Tyne and Nottingham.

Wages system
Computerisation has done much to take the drudgery out of running the wages side of a business. But it still needs three main elements: the equivalent of a *Wages book* as an overall record, an individual record for each employee to inspect, and the advice note to go to each employee with their pay or when it is transferred to their bank accounts.

Warrant
A warrant is an assurance or guarantee. On the Stock Exchange, it is a document guaranteeing that its owner can buy shares in a company at a fixed price – making it a type of *Option*.

Warranty See *Guarantee*.

Wasting asset
An asset with a limited life, with a shrinking value during that life.
   For tax purposes, it has to be a life of less than 50 years. That makes plant and machinery wasting assets, as are property leases of less than 50 years.

Wealth

Wealth is lots of something we want to have lots of, whether
it be beauty, truth, flowers, trees or wads of green folding
stuff. Personal wealth tends to mean large houses
surrounded by expensive toys, such as cars, boats, planes,
lakes and parkland. Oh, and islands. Some believe that no
one should have so much, which is why wealth is a
politically explosive subject. See also *National wealth*.

Wealth tax

Wealth tax is a regular assessment – in practice, it would
probably be yearly – of individuals' wealth. If they were found
to have more than a certain amount, then they would have
to hand some of it over to the government. In the 1970s,
a House of Commons committee looked into the prospects
for introducing a wealth tax, but the eventual report was split
at least three ways. Since then the subject has been dropped,
but it is likely to return from time to time.

Weather insurance

If you are running a fête or a street party, it can be both
annoying and expensive to have it rained off. But it is possible
to insure against a certain amount of rain falling on any
open-air event. The leading insurer of weather risks is
Eagle Star, which operates what it calls a *Pluvius* policy,
Eagle Star's head office is at 1 Threadneedle Street,
London EC2R 8BE, but there are branches round the
country.

Welsh

A piece of nineteenth-century slang, meaning to cheat on a
bet by refusing to pay. Gambling debts are not enforceable in
law. Over the years the term has been widened to include
cheating on any financial deal. Someone who welshes is a
welsher.

Whole life insurance

Like *Term insurance*, Whole life is a cheap form of life

insurance in that it offers reasonable cover for a modest premium. Unlike term insurance, it is a bet on a certainty – that the 'life', the person named on the policy, will die eventually. The only risk, from the insurer's point of view, is that the person will die sooner rather than later. Otherwise, it is a backstop form of investment, giving a nest-egg to the 'life's' dependents. See *Life insurance*.

Wholesale
The sale of the whole of a batch of goods, as against to selling them piecemeal by *Retail*. Goods bought wholesale are cheaper because of the savings in labour, transport and paperwork costs, but most members of the public cannot afford to buy more than small amounts at one time.

Wholesale banking
This is concerned with large-scale finance, normally involving other banks or large organisations such as companies and local authorities. Because of the sums being dealt in, wholesale banking bypasses the extra costs of dealing in small amounts with the general public. That is called *Retail banking*.

Widowed mother's allowance
An extension of the *Widow's allowance*. It is payable if she is living with a child under 19, for whom she is paid *Child benefit*. The child must have been born of the widow and her late husband, or the widow and late husband must have been living together at the time of death. It is also payable to pregnant widows, but does depend on the husband's National Insurance payments.

Widow's allowance See *Widow's pension*.

Widow's bereavement allowance
This is a special tax allowance paid to a widow in the year her husband dies – if he had been entitled to the *Married man's allowance*. The allowance is trimmed for each month

of the *Fiscal year* which had elapsed prior to the husband's
death. See *Death grant, Industrial death*.

Widow's pension
Anyone who is unfortunate enough to be widowed should
go – or send someone on her behalf – as soon as possible
to the local social security office, which appears in most
phone books under 'Health and Social Security, Dept.
of'. The rules on allowances and pensions for widows are
complex and liable to change, and a batch of up-to-date
leaflets is essential reading. See also *Widow's bereavement
allowance*.

Wife's earned income allowance
This is a device designed to stop couples avoiding tax by
putting investments in the wife's name. When a woman
marries, she continues in that tax year to have the *Single
person's allowance* set against her taxable income – whether
from work or investments. But after the next 6 April, the
wife's earned income allowance comes into play. This has
always been identical to the single person's allowance: the
only difference is that it does not help to cut tax on income
from investments. It also plays a part in the process of
Separate assessment.

Will
A formal statement of how someone wants his possessions
to be disposed of after his death. If you do not make a
will, the law steps in and distributes your property according
to a laid-down formula which may not suit you. If you do
not want to go to a solicitor, legal stationery shops sell
do-it-yourself will kits, or you can consult your local
Citizens' Advice Bureau. See *Devise, Executor, Legacy*.

Wilson Report
Officially known as the Commission to Review the
Functioning of Financial Institutions, Cmnd 7937, it was set
up by James Callaghan in 1976. Callaghan appointed Sir

Harold (now Lord) Wilson to chair the committee, which
surveyed banks, building societies, insurance companies,
pension funds, the stock market, public sector finance,
the Bank of England, and other nationalised industries. The
report, published in 1980, criticised the pension funds as
not being sufficiently accountable to their members or to
the public. It points out that building societies were
growing and might have to be brought under control, and
it argues that outsiders should be allowed to sit on the
Stock Exchange Council.

With-profits insurance

Most *Life insurance* policies come in two basic forms: with
profits and without. *Whole life* and *Term insurance* are typical
kinds of without-profits policy. In each case you agree a
premium and a benefit, both of which are fixed. The
benefit may or may not include some interest on your
premiums over the period. Either way, if inflation
suddenly rockets after you have signed up, you will get
nothing extra. With-profits policies do pay extra during
the period of the policy, however. The main type here is
Endowment insurance. A guaranteed sum is agreed at the
start, usually equal to little more than the total value of your
premiums. Then, every one to three years, a bonus is
added to that guaranteed sum, expressed as a percentage on
your previous guarantee. Once added, it cannot be taken
away. At the end, some insurers will add a terminal bonus.
The tricky question is whether those bonuses will be big
enough to offset the extra premiums you pay for the
with-profits policy. See also *Unit-linked insurance*.

Won

Korea was divided after the second world war into North
and South zones, under the wing of the USSR and US
respectively. They have both continued to call their
currencies the won, but the two have diverged dramatically.
In the south, the won is quite freely traded at 1,300 to the

pound. The North Korean won is forbidden to be imported or exported, and it is worth about 60p.

Work in progress
Depending how lengthy a production process is, goods can spend a considerable time in a state of limbo between being raw materials and finished goods. In this state, they would be much harder to sell than at either end of the conveyor belt. In a healthy business, they are valued at their factory cost, which includes some *Overheads*.

Working capital
The money that is used to pay for the day-to-day running of the business, as opposed to the fixed assets. It goes to buying raw materials, pays the workers' wages and the fuel bills, as well as any extras like the chairman's Earl Grey tea.

Working capital ratio
This is simply a company's *Current assets* divided by its *Current liabilities*, to see whether a company is sufficiently liquid. The sum should produce an answer of two or more, but the safe ratio varies from industry to industry. See also *Acid test, Current ratio*.

World Bank
An independent agency of the United Kingdom, the World Bank was set up by the *Bretton Woods* agreement. Initially it was concerned with helping countries to recover from the second world war. Now, however, it is more involved in funnelling money from rich countries to poor ones, on loans lasting officially up to about 20 years. Really poor countries can get cheap loans through the bank's International Development Association, and private investment is encouraged through another arm, the International Finance Corporation. The bank's formal name and London address is the International Bank for Reconstruction and Development, New Zealand House, 80 Haymarket, London SW1Y 4TE.

Writing-down allowance

This is a method of allowing the cost of plant and machinery, and buildings, against tax. But the two categories must be considered separately. A percentage of the outstanding cost of plant and machinery is allowed each year, after deducting the *First-year allowance*. This is the 'reducing balance' method. Industrial buildings are allowed on a straight-line basis: the same amount is allowed each year, so long as the building is owned and in use on the last day of the period.

Xu

Vietnam's smallest currency unit. There are 10 xu to the hao, and 100 xu to the dong.

Yankee bond *See Bulldog bond.*

Yearling bonds

Issued by local authorities, these bonds are repaid in full after a year, with accrued interest. As the interest can be treated as capital gain, there is often less tax to pay than on other comparable investments. This can make yearlings attractive to higher-rate tax payers.

Yen

Adopted in 1875, the yen is Japan's currency. Originally equal to a US dollar, there are now about 170 to the dollar, and 260 to the pound. But the rate has been coming down as the Japanese economic miracle has unfolded. A sign of this is that Tokyo has become one of the most expensive cities in the world for foreigners.

Yield

This says, as a percentage, how many pence you will get on every pound you put into a particular investment. In a gilt-edged stock it may be 15%. On a share it could be anything from 1% upwards. On a bar of gold it is 0%. Shares can be confusing, as dividends are often shown as a percentage of their par value, a figure of interest only to accountants and probably bearing no relation to the price you paid. You can convert by multiplying the dividend percentage by the par value – it is on your share certificate – and then dividing the result by the price you paid.

Youth Opportunities Programme
This was a scheme run by the *Manpower Services Commission* to give young unemployed people a taste of work, with the hope that they might pick up some skills into the bargain and maybe even turn the job into a full-timer. Some employers were criticised for using the scheme to get cheap labour. See *Project Fullemploy, Youth Training Scheme*.

Youth Training Scheme
Successor to the *Manpower Service Commission's Youth Opportunities Programme*. It is designed to give 16-year-old school leavers two years' basic training in job skills. As time goes on it will be offered to older people and link up with job creation projects. See also *Project Fullemploy*.

Yuan
China's principal currency unit, worth about 30p. It is divided into 10 jiao and 100 fen. Yuan notes are issued in numbers from one to 10, and it is pronounced 'kuai'.

Zaire
Zaire's currency unit, worth about 2p.

Zero coupon bond
A *Bond* which has no coupon, meaning that it does not pay a dividend. What the investor gets is an inbuilt capital gain. The bond is issued at a low price, perhaps £30, but will be redeemed for £100. The investor pays no capital gains tax on the profit, but he is liable to income tax on the dividends he would have otherwise received.

Zero-rating   280

Zero-rating

Under the *Value-Added Tax* rules, certain basic goods and services are not charged VAT. They include most food, sewerage and water services, books and newspapers, fuel and power, construction, some international services and all exports. However, there is plenty of small print in this list, and anyone who wants the full details should write to the *Customs and Excise Department*, King's Beam House, Mark Lane, London EC3R 7HE. See also *Exempt*.

Zloty

Poland's currency unit since 1923, coming from the Polish for gold. There are about 170 to the pound, but there has been strong exchange control.

Z-score

A method of predicting if a company is going to go bust. It is based on analysis of balance sheets over a period of years, observing the trends in *Cash flow*, *Stock turnover*, *Current ratio* and *Debt-equity ratio*. The art lies in the relative weight given to these factors. Few of the experts are willing to discuss their calculations because of the risk of libel, and because by publishing such a prediction a company's creditors could demand their money, hastening a collapse.

282

Bibliography

ALLEN: *Your Taxes and Saving In Retirement* (Age Concern, 1979)

AUGHTON: *Housing Finance: a Basic Guide* (Shelter, 1981)

BERTRAM and EDWARDS: *Comprehensive Aspects of Taxation* (Cassell, 1982)

COOPERS and LYBRAND: *Tax Saving for the Family Business* (Harrap, 1982)

FINGLETON and TICKELL: *The Penguin Book of Money* (Penguin, 1980)

GLEESON: *The Credit Book* (Kogan Page, 1982)

HANSON: *Moneyguide: the handbook of personal finance* (Kluwer, 1981)

Investors Chronicle: *Beginners Please* (Eyre Methuen, 1975)

WHITEHEAD: *Bookkeeping Made Simple* (Heinemann, 1981)